THE COMMONWEALTH DAY HANDBOOK FOR SCHOOLS

Compiled by Wendy Davis

Education Programme
Human Resource Development Group
Commonwealth Secretariat
Marlborough House, Pall Mall, London SW1Y 5HX

Front Cover Photograph: Zurrieq Primary School 'A'. Malta.
Commonwealth Day 1985

CONTENTS

THE MODERN COMMONWEALTH

Tuvalu

Kiribati

Nauru

Solomon Islands

Vanuatu

New Zealand

Australia

Papua New Guinea

Brunei

Malaysia

Singapore

Bangladesh

Sri Lanka

India

Maldives

Seychelles

Mauritius

Kenya

Uganda

Tanzania

Malawi

Zambia

Zimbabwe

Botswana

Swaziland

Lesotho

Cyprus

Malta

Britain

Nigeria

The Gambia

Sierra Leone

Ghana

St Kitts & Nevis

Antigua & Barbuda

Dominica

St Lucia

Barbados

St Vincent & the Grenadines

Grenada

Trinidad & Tobago

The Bahamas

Jamaica

Belize

Guyana

Canada

Western Samoa

Tonga

PREFACE

On Monday 14 March 1977, I joined many young Ghanaians in Accra in celebrating the first Commonwealth Day. It was a day of learning and enjoyment; a day to symbolise the emotional and practical ties which unite a quarter of the world's population through the Commonwealth.

Just two years earlier, Heads of Government, meeting in Kingston, Jamaica had expressed support for a proposal that there should be simultaneous observance of Commonwealth Day in all Commonwealth countries. Subsequently, the second Monday in March was identified as being one of those days in the calendar when schools everywhere in the Commonwealth would be in session. This choice reflected the belief that Commonwealth Day should not be a holiday, but a day of local activities, through schools and communities, which would express the principles and ideals of the Commonwealth in practical form.

Now, twelve years later, we have accumulated an impressive record of how Commonwealth Day has been celebrated in the schools, colleges and communities of our member states. This handbook shares that experience for the benefit of all those interested in ensuring that the ideals and work of the Commonwealth are handed on to those who will see it into the twenty-first century. At the same time, it has been prepared in recognition of the fact that for many teachers and students, information about the Commonwealth is not always easy to obtain, especially for those of you working in rural schools, perhaps with limited resources. This handbook has been designed with you very much in mind. If it helps to stimulate an awareness of the wider world in which the young have an important co-operative role to play, it will have served its purpose.

Commonwealth Secretary-General

ACKNOWLEDGEMENTS

The Commonwealth Secretariat acknowledges the assistance given by Margaret Brayton, Sheila Davies, Greg Gardner, Tony Humphries, Derek Ingram and Trevor Williams in the compilation of this handbook.

The line drawings were prepared by Karen Douglas (pp. 17, 21, 23, 25, 86).

The Secretariat appreciates the permission given to allow the use of copyright material:

World Studies Project - Images of Peace (p.42)
Peace Education Project - Co-operation Squares (p.48)
Birmingham Development Education Centre - Brainstorming (p.11)
Child-to-child Programme - Health Activities (pp.64-69)

Photographs:

Antonia Reeve Photography (p.2 - Tongan dancers)
All-Sport Photographic Ltd (p.28 Ben Johnson and p.29)
John Mulaka (p.52)
United Nations (p.79)
Commonwealth Youth Exchange Council (p.88)

1
INTRODUCTION

Tongan dancers with Royal Tongan Police Band at Commonwealth Arts Festival.

Nigerian Artists at the Commonwealth Institute in London.

ABOUT THIS HANDBOOK

Why a handbook for schools?

Commonwealth Day - the second Monday in March - falls on a school day in virtually every Commonwealth country. The date was chosen deliberately so that schools everywhere could take part in the observances and celebrations. Since 1977 schools all over the Commonwealth have organised special activities designed to enhance understanding of the Commonwealth and to provide shared enjoyment. The purpose of this handbook is to build on the initiatives of recent years and to propose further ideas which can extend the scope of schools' activities.

Who is the handbook for?

The handbook is intended for educators who are concerned with teaching about the Commonwealth: Commonwealth Desk Officers in Ministries of Education; those involved in curriculum development; and teachers in secondary, junior and infant schools. An educational level is suggested for each activity in the handbook.

What is it about?

This handbook offers ideas and projects focused on Commonwealth Day to stimulate interest in the Commonwealth and enhance study of it. The handbook takes the approach that Commonwealth Day activities will have greater meaning and value if they form part of longer-term work or take place as the culmination of projects carried out over the previous weeks. Learning about the Commonwealth is clearly not something that can be done in one day. As Secretary-General Shridath Ramphal has implied: "I would like every day to be Commonwealth Day so that we can talk more about it. I would like to reach more of the people, more of the young people of the Commonwealth so that they become part of our process of information."

Information is not always easy to come by. The majority of schools in the Commonwealth have limited access to books and other media through which information about the rest of the world, including the Commonwealth, is transmitted. This handbook includes a number of activities that do not depend on these wider resources but which, instead, draw on the human and material resources of the school and the community. Communication and the sharing of information and skills are as essential at the local level as they are in international affairs; socially useful activities involving different members of the school and the community can therefore give practical expression to the principles of co-operation and sharing by which the Commonwealth is guided.

What kind of activities?

The projects outlined in the handbook are of four main kinds:

> Country projects or topic work, which explore aspects of the Commonwealth's cultural diversity;

> Activity-based study of Commonwealth principles, such as the right of people to live in peace or to be free from racial discrimination;

> Learning about the evolution of the modern Commonwealth;

> Learning about the way Commonwealth governments, organisations and peoples work together - linked to practical local work based on co-operation.

In each case specific suggestions are made for exhibitions, performances and other activities to take place on Commonwealth Day itself. It is hoped that schools will make Commonwealth Day an Open Day to which parents and other members of the community are invited. The school may listen to the Queen's Commonwealth Day message and to messages from the Head of State or Minister of Education, as well as holding some kind of formal multi-faith observance; but equally important is the opportunity to mark the success or endeavour of projects in the school and the community, to enjoy exhibitions and performances, debates and games and to celebrate informally.

A full list of the activities and projects in this handbook can be found on p.106.

2
RECENT COMMONWEALTH DAY ACTIVITIES IN SCHOOLS

The Commonwealth Secretariat often receives reports from schools of their Commonwealth Day activities and celebrations. Quotes from some of their reports and brief descriptions of events organised appear on the next three pages.

COMMONWEALTH DAY EVENTS

The 'Queen' welcomes delegates at a student
Heads of Government meeting in Tanzania.

Commonwealth display by
Antiguan school children.

Western Australia Governor with
winner of Commonwealth speech and
leadership contest.

Commonwealth Day event in India – a dance from Bihar.

Sunnyside School Antigua

"After a week of tropical depressions and uncertain weather (Sahara dust, some said) the morning of March 11th dawned bright and clear - lovely blue skies and no wind. This is very important to us at Sunnyside as we have no Assembly Hall and all our special programmes are performed in the open air, our stage being what is left of the balcony of a ruined sugar plantation estate house. The audience sit in the shade of the classroom huts and trees. With everyone in colourful traditional costume we looked a truly Commonwealth gathering. Countries represented ranged from the founder members to the newest members and the largest to the smallest nations. Assembly items included songs, poetry, dance, mime, skits, celebrations, history and information. Two members of staff wrote poems especially for the occasion. After the assembly everyone visited the classroom displays and saw maps, paintings, produce, stamps, souvenirs, shells, plants, models, clothes, newspapers, slides, photographs, books, leaflets, food, listened to music from Jamaica, tasted rice chicken and poppodoms from India, and Red Herring, Johnnie Cakes and Potato Pie from Antigua, drank soursop and tamarind drinks and thoroughly enjoyed themselves. Many photographs were taken and prizes were awarded for the best displays, costumes and special efforts.

Nigeria

"In one school the members of a dramatic society put on a short play. The theme was the importance of living in harmony with our neighbours. The title was "Unity in Diversity."

Cayman Islands

"All Government schools planted trees, namely Ficus and Neeme. During the ceremonies officials read the Queen's Speech which was directed to Commonwealth youth. The children were reminded that the trees planted would grow to be large and useful just like the Commonwealth which has grown to be a large, useful organisation.

Malta

"In one school 24 students from different Commonwealth countries toured classes, dressed in traditional costumes, and spoke about customs and daily life in their respective countries.

A Primary school sent over 500 special messages to children in 20 Commonwealth countries.

A Home Economics class prepared 20 different delicacies from as many different countries. A secondary school mounted an exhibition of newspapers and children's magazines from the Commonwealth."

"A very popular item was the flag raising ceremony. Flags of the different member countries were hoisted simultaneously, by children wearing the national costumes of the countries whose flags they were hoisting."

"May the wind carry our friendship to all the people of the Commonwealth." Message on a streamer in a kite and balloon flying event.

Uganda

"On Sunday 8 March (the day before Commonwealth Day) the television featured a panel discussion on the Commonwealth. Two schools contested in a quiz about the Commonwealth. This was televised on Commonwealth Day at night. The programmes were also broadcast on the radio."

Sri Lanka

"Sri Lanka being a multiracial country, the message of the Commonwealth was conveyed with great enthusiasm. The accent was on the help rendered by other Commonwealth countries to build up the economy."

Union Methodist School, St Vincent and the Grenadines

"The Infants' presentation was entitled "The Commonwealth - Each Other's Helper." The message supporting the theme was - "In the Commonwealth we help each other by trading." Pupils represented ships carrying cargo from one country to another. On their heads they carried boxes displaying the products. By the end of the exercise none of the ships was at its home base (this being represented by another pupil with the name of the country displayed on his/her chest)."

"Junior 5 presented "Extracts from speeches of outstanding Commonwealth figures." These included words of the late Dr Eric Williams concerning the break-up of the Federation, words of Indira Gandhi on non-alignment, and words of the Calypsonian of the world - Mighty Sparrow - urging school children to grasp every opportunity for learning."

Zimbabwe

"Some of the outstanding performances were traditional dances of some neighbouring Commonwealth countries such as Malawi, Zambia and Botswana. The singers were dressed in the traditional attire of these countries."

The Bahamas

"Assemblies followed themes of peace and unity. Special studies were undertaken on famous statesmen, writers and national festivals. One school organised a Commonwealth arts and craft competition. Guest speakers from other Commonwealth countries were invited to schools."

3
MAKING A START

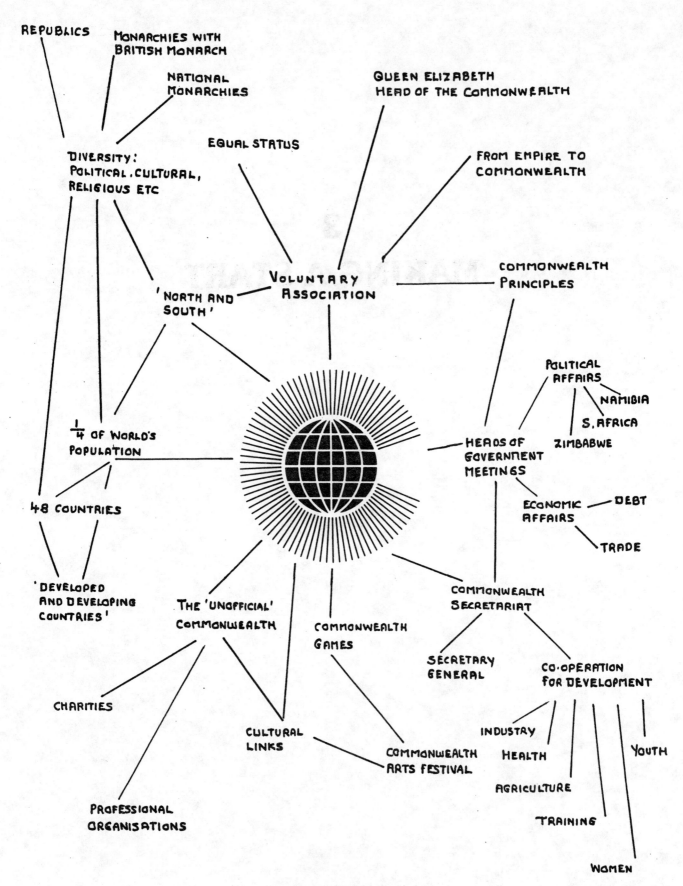

REPUBLICS

MONARCHIES WITH
BRITISH MONARCH

NATIONAL
MONARCHIES

QUEEN ELIZABETH
HEAD OF THE COMMONWEALTH

EQUAL STATUS

DIVERSITY:
POLITICAL, CULTURAL,
RELIGIOUS ETC

FROM EMPIRE TO
COMMONWEALTH

'NORTH AND
SOUTH'

VOLUNTARY
ASSOCIATION

COMMONWEALTH
PRINCIPLES

POLITICAL
AFFAIRS

NAMIBIA

S. AFRICA

ZIMBABWE

1/4 OF WORLD'S
POPULATION

HEADS OF
GOVERNMENT
MEETINGS

ECONOMIC
AFFAIRS

DEBT

TRADE

48 COUNTRIES

'DEVELOPED
AND DEVELOPING
COUNTRIES'

THE 'UNOFFICIAL'
COMMONWEALTH

COMMONWEALTH
GAMES

COMMONWEALTH
SECRETARIAT

SECRETARY
GENERAL

CO-OPERATION
FOR DEVELOPMENT

CHARITIES

CULTURAL
LINKS

COMMONWEALTH
ARTS FESTIVAL

INDUSTRY

HEALTH

YOUTH

AGRICULTURE

PROFESSIONAL
ORGANISATIONS

TRAINING

WOMEN

A COMMONWEALTH WEB

Rather than starting preparation for Commonwealth Day by giving students a set of facts about the Commonwealth, it is a good idea to find out how much they already know. The following activity gives students an opportunity to identify and share existing knowledge. It gives everyone a chance to contribute and helps create an atmosphere of co-operation and confidence. It also gives students an overview of the theme to be studied.

Activity 1(a): BRAINSTORMING   **Level: Secondary**

Ask the students in a limited space of time (say 5-10 minutes) to come up with as many ideas as possible on the subject of the Commonwealth. This can be done by students working in small groups and reporting back to the class, or by the class as a whole, with the teacher or a student recording the ideas on a poster or blackboard. It is important for every idea to be accepted without discussion at this stage, no matter how far fetched it might appear.

Questions that could provide useful starting points are:

    What comes to mind when you think of the Commonwealth?
    What do you associate with the Commonwealth?

When as many ideas as possible have been collected, students could be asked to try grouping or linking them in the form of a web (see p.10). The implications of the ideas can then be discussed, e.g. the ideas may indicate that:

    The Commonwealth has a history;
    The Commonwealth links together people from all over the world;
    It is concerned with co-operation (consultation/training/ development).

After the discussion the teacher can show the class a large poster of a 'Commonwealth web' which has been prepared in advance (see p.10). It is important to emphasise that the teacher's chart does not represent the only 'right' response to the brainstorming exercise. The students will have thought of valid ideas that do not appear on the poster. The web which the teacher may have adapted from the one shown here, depending on the age and circumstances of the students, simply serves to take the students' ideas a stage further, to reinforce their existing knowledge and to open up new aspects of the subject which they did not previously know about.

Students can then be invited to ask questions about the 'Commonwealth web'. The answers need not be very extended but can give a taste of further areas of study that may be explored in the coming weeks.

Activity 1(b): BRAINSTORMING   Level: Primary

For younger children it may be too difficult to look at the Commonwealth as an entity and as an association that works in particular ways. A more appropriate subject for the brainstorming exercise may therefore be an individual Commonwealth country rather than the Commonwealth as a whole.

Alternatively, students can be asked to write down as many Commonwealth countries as they can think of and anything else they know about the Commonwealth. This can be followed by a discussion in which pupils share their ideas and knowledge and the teacher can begin to introduce topics for further study and project work.

Activity 2: DETECTIVE WORK   Level Junior/secondary

Either as a follow-up to the 'brainstorming' activity or as an alternative activity, ask the students to find out as much as they can about the Commonwealth before the next lesson. Ask them to see what they can find out from their parents, relations or other members of the community, from the school library, and from local churches, post offices or other institutions. Can they bring any 'evidence' of what they have found out?

When the students have put their pieces of information and evidence together, what conclusions can they draw and what further things do they as 'detectives' need to find out before they can understand what the Commonwealth is about?

4
ONE COMMONWEALTH, MANY PEOPLES

Commonwealth Secretary-General Shridath Ramphal with staff of the Commonwealth Secretariat.

ONE COMMONWEALTH, MANY PEOPLES

Commonwealth Day provides a good opportunity for presentations and exhibitions which demonstrate the diversity of environments, cultures and traditions of Commonwealth peoples who together make up a quarter of the world's population. Classroom preparation can take place in Geography, History, English, Social Studies, Religion and Arts and Crafts lessons or, ideally, within an integrated curriculum.

The level of conceptualisation required in this area of study, together with the need for a reasonably flexible structure, make it particularly suitable for primary and junior schools, or for the younger end of the secondary school.

There are two main approaches:

A   Projects on individual Commonwealth countries;

B   Theme or topic work related to the Commonwealth generally or to a particular region, e.g. Caribbean, Asia, Pacific.

The limitation of the country- or topic-based approach is that it does not necessarily of itself lead to an understanding of the Commonwealth as a whole. If teachers are able to combine this kind of work with some of the activities and information in other sections of this handbook, pupils should be able to gain a clearer idea of what the Commonwealth means and what it is in practice. In the study of a particular theme or country the Commonwealth connection should anyway be drawn out wherever possible.

A. COUNTRY PROJECTS   Level: Junior/lower secondary

It is best to choose countries about which it is relatively easy to find information. Pupils may work separately on their chosen countries or in small groups on joint projects, or the whole class may work together in studying a particular country. If the whole class studies one country, it is helpful for other classes to take different countries, perhaps from different regions, so that a fair range is covered by the school as a whole and a varied display can be mounted for Commonwealth Day.

The project could include all or some of the following:

*   Looking at pupils' own images and sterotypes - establishing their existing perceptions.

*   Checking their images against some basic geographical and social information.

*   Looking up equivalent information about their own country and trying to identify similarities and differences. (This comparative approach could usefully be adopted throughout the course of project work).

*   Using photographs. Here it is important that wherever possible pictures of countries should balance poverty and affluence, urban and rural, modern and traditional.

*   Investigation of geography. Map work.

*   Study of a society through modern short stories, autobiographical accounts, poems, folk tales.

*   Study of where people live. Wide variety and standard of houses. Existence of homelessness in all societies.

*   Study of vegetation and crops. How people meet basic needs of foods and clothing. Learning recipes. Making clothes.

*   Learning about the country's wildlife. Young children will enjoy doing drawings and paintings.

*   Brief introduction to important historical events (including becoming member of the Commonwealth).

*   Learning about the main religions and their effect on the society.

*   Art and craft work.

*   Dance, drama and song.

The project will be given a new dimension if a national from the country studied, or someone who knows the country well, is able to participate in the work and share their first-hand knowledge and experience. This too may require a bit of 'detective work'. The Ministry of Education may be able to help with contact addresses for overseas teachers. Churches, hospitals, and foreign companies operating locally, are other possible sources.

School links

The best way of learning about another Commonwealth country is by making direct links. Students can be encouraged to write to pen friends and exchange information, pictures, photos, news etc. Alternatively, or in addition, a special link can be made with a school in another Commonwealth country. The Commonwealth Linking Trust (see p.104) helps put schools in touch with each other and many schools have found this an enriching experience.

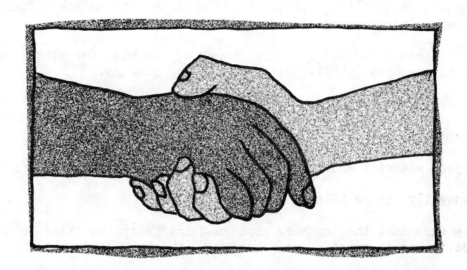

Starting a link: a teacher's advice

The essence of a successful school exchange of correspondence lies in the relationship, aims and objectives of the teachers concerned. If a school exchange is to fit into a course containing a wide variety of activities a number of points should be tackled at the outset:

*   Each school should try to appreciate the exact relevance of the exchange in the other school's curriculum.

*   The actual nature of the exchange should be agreed. (Is it to be a one-to-one pen-friendship, or a general exchange of individual work, or an exchange of group-based project work?).

*   The frequency of the exchange should be discussed. Ideally, an actual timetable of delivery dates, preferably for the whole school year, should be agreed upon by both parties.

*   The expected duration of the exchange between any two groups or classes should be agreed. One year may well be a suitable initial period.

Many kinds of items can be exchanged:

* Diaries of life in the two schools/communities.

* Copies of school magazines and newsletters.

* Tapes of songs and stories, and messages from pupils.

* Photographs of students, their families and school activities.

* Drawings and paintings of the local environment: people, homes, trees, flowers, animals, insects, everyday scenes.

* Small items collected locally: pieces of material for clothing, unusual pebbles, shells, dried leaves and flowers.

* Collections of stories, legends and folk tales.

* Scrapbooks.

* Project material and descriptions of Commonwealth Day celebrations.

More generally, it is helpful to:

* Make sure that the teachers concerned are fully committed to the undertaking in practice, not merely in theory.

* Put the exchange as a first priority. Alter lesson schedules to adapt to the exchange as the need arises.

* Be prepared to devote a considerable amount of time to preparing the best material from your pupils for the exchange. Hurriedly executed work does not help to establish a good correspondence - or mutual appreciation.

* Remember to allow adequate lesson time for the packages received, especially if the exchange is an integral part of a syllabus. Analysis and appreciation of a package can be a lengthy procedure if it is to be worthwhile.

* Try to link up children of approximately the same age.

* Determine at the outset whether the other school is seeking an exchange of visits following the correspondence.

* If an eventual exchange of visits is agreed, determine at the outset the exact number of your own pupils interested in accommodating visiting correspondents in their own home. Volunteers sometimes fade into the background when the time arrives.

* Keep the exchange school informed about any alterations to the original schedule (e.g. a package being unavoidably late).

It is helpful not to:

* Promise your pupils anything about the exchange which is not absolutely certain. It can undermine credibility.

* Assume that the teacher with whom you have established an exchange is agreeing with your suggestion unless it is actually specified (e.g. that your correspondents are prepared to complete and return the questionnaires devised by your own pupils).

* Be too ambitious about how many packages you want to exchange each term. If they are to be the best quality your pupils can achieve, they will take a surprising length of time to put together.

(This list is based on the experience of a teacher who has developed school links).

On Commonwealth Day

* Country projects will provide the basis for a varied and colourful exhibition of maps, charts, written work, drawings, craft work etc. If a link with a school in another Commonwealth country has been formed, the display can include letters, photographs and other materials received from the link school.

* Dances, songs, and drama can be performed.

B. THEME/TOPIC WORK   Level: Infant/junior/lower secondary

Almost any theme or topic can be explored cross-culturally and used to demonstrate the diversity that exists within the Commonwealth. Topic work is more valuable if the aim is not merely to 'collect examples' of different customs or facets of life in Commonwealth countries but also to look at the factors that give rise to this diversity. In this way, children are helped to see other cultures as not just different - or worse still, exotic or alien - but as the specific ways in which human beings, who are fundamentally the same in their needs, hopes, abilities and feelings, have responded to the various circum- stances and conditions of life they find themselves in.

The topics that follow are just a handful from the many ideas that could be explored.

FOOD   Literature   Clothes

RELIGIONS   SHELTER

TRANSPORT   Art and Craft

FOOD

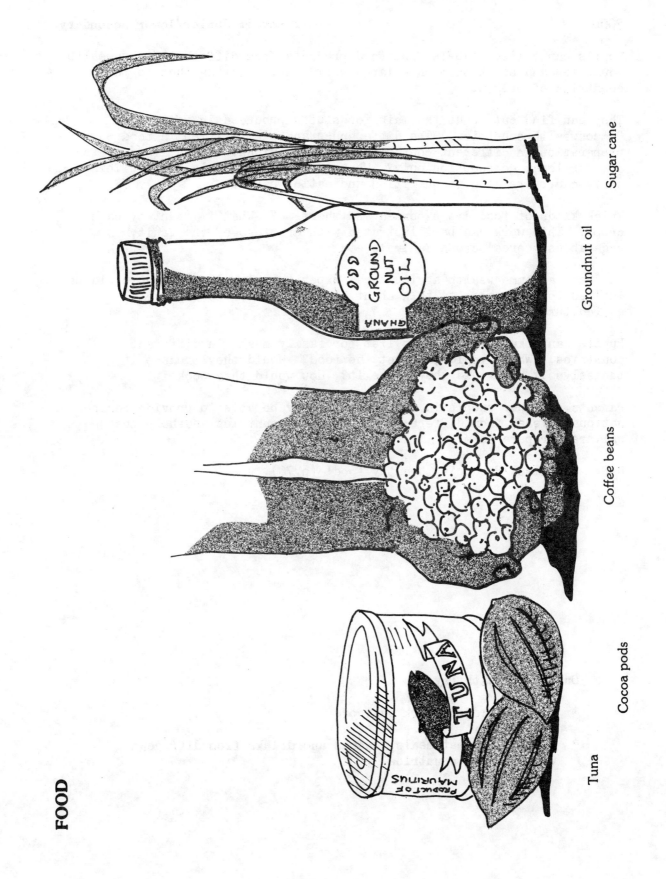

Sugar cane

Groundnut oil

Coffee beans

Tuna

Cocoa pods

Pupils can collect labels from food products from different Commonwealth countries and stick them on a large world map, relating them to their countries of origin.

They can find out about the main foodstuffs produced in various Commonwealth countries. The differences and similarities in food preparation in different countries can be examined. Which kinds of food are for local consumption only? What is meant by staple foods? This study can be related to nutrition and eating habits.

Which kinds of food are exported and where to? What is meant by cash crops? This work can be illustrated with drawings of the fruit, vegetables, cereal crops, animals etc.

Is there a Commonwealth agricultural expert working locally who could be invited to the school to talk about his or her work to improve agricultural production?

Pupils can make up a shopping list for family meals in different countries. Where would they get the food? Would they produce it themselves? How would they store it? How would they cook it?

Parents or other people in the community may be able to provide recipes of national dishes from different Commonwealth countries and help the children prepare them.

N.B. See also 'Producing healthy food' (p.70).

On Commonwealth Day

* **Display project work on food**

* **Prepare and eat meals, snacks and drinks from different Commonwealth countries**

CLOTHES

An Indian Sari.

Pupils can find out about clothes worn by different Commonwealth peoples.
They can discuss the differences and similarities between clothes worn in
their own country and in other Commonwealth countries. They can cut out
pictures from magazines, look for illustrations and descriptions of
clothes in library books (encyclopedias, stories etc.) and make colourful
drawings and paintings of them in art classes. Small children may like to
dress up dolls and puppets in national dress made from scraps of
materials.

Discuss the design of clothes with children. Look at everyday working
clothes as well as clothes for special occasions. In what way are the
clothes practical, suitable for particular types of work or for particular
weather conditions? Is there any connection between religious belief and
the style and design of clothes? How is individuality expressed through
the clothes people wear? Compare women's and men's clothing. Discuss the
influence of fashion.

Parents or other people from different Commonwealth countries can be
invited to demonstrate how clothes are worn.

Clothes can be made from scraps of cloth, paper, old sheets etc. Use
silver foil, bottle tops, seeds and other small objects as jewellery.
Experiment with printing, dyeing and embroidery.

On Commonwealth Day

Pupils can dress up in the clothes they have made. They can
put on a parade for visitors and as each pupils walks across
the stage another pupil can briefly explain why the clothes
are designed as they are.

Display project work on Commonwealth clothes.

CLOTHES

West African Styles.

CREATIVE ARTS   **Level: Infant/junior/lower secondary**

There is plenty of scope for enjoyable learning about the literature,
drama, art and music of Commonwealth countries and for attractive
presentations on Commonwealth Day:

*   Younger children will enjoy traditional folk tales from different
    parts of the Commonwealth.

*   Children could make wall friezes, cartoons and paintings to illustrate
    the stories. Some stories may lend themselves to dramatisation.

*   Older students may be able, with the help of teachers and local
    libraries, to mount an exhibition of fiction by modern Commonwealth
    writers.

*   Depending on the availability of books and other resources, a study of
    the arts, crafts and architecture of other Commonwealth countries
    could be made. If artefacts can be brought into the classroom the
    experience will be a more real and immediate one. Musical
    instruments, printing blocks, decorated calabashes, ceremonial objects
    etc. can be used or experimented with and can also serve as models for
    many forms of craft work.

*   Children can learn songs and dances from different Commonwealth
    countries. As with other themes, it may be possible to invite
    nationals to teach these to the pupils.

   On Commonwealth Day

   *   Put on exhibitions and performances.

   *   Dramatic presentations could combine various art forms.
       Plays based on Commonwealth stories may include dance and
       song, and art and craft work may provide some of the props
       and scenery.

CREATIVE ARTS

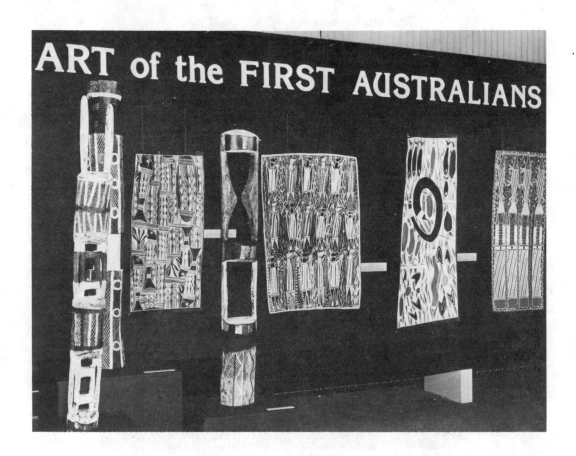

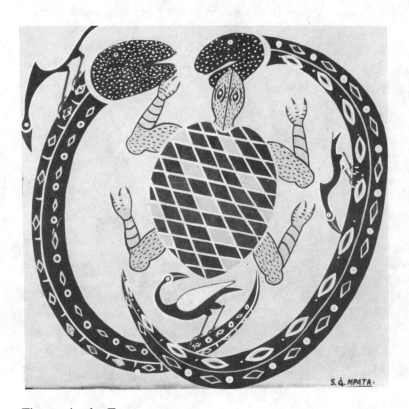

The work of a Tanzanian artist.

GAMES AND SPORT

Canadian athlete Ben Johnson at the Commonwealth Games.

Australian surf rides.

Jeff Dujon (West Indies) appeals for wicket of Mike Gatting (England). Reliance World Cup 1987.

GAMES AND SPORT　　　　　　　　　　　**Level: Infant/junior secondary**

Pupils may be able to find out about various games and sports played in different Commonwealth countries. Which of these have become common in many or all Commonwealth countries or have similarities with games played elsewhere?

Children who come from, or have lived in, other Commonwealth countries could teach some popular children's games to the others.

Project work could be done on the Commonwealth Games: information on notable events, record holders, numbers of competitors etc; drawings of sportsmen and women; discussions on Commonwealth action on sporting links with South Africa.

The Commonwealth Games

The Commonwealth Games began in 1930 as the 'British Empire Games' and have been held every four years since then. Numbers of competitors have risen from 400 in 1930 to 1583 in 1982. The Games feature up to ten events which always include athletics and swimming - the other eight being selected from archery, badminton, bowls, boxing, canoeing, cycling, fencing, gymnastics, judo, rowing, shooting, table-tennis, weight-lifting and yachting. Contestants must be amateurs and are accommodated in a special Commonwealth Games village for the duration of the Games. A Commonwealth arts festival coinciding with the Games is normally organised by the host country.

The 13th Commonwealth Games was in Edinburgh, Scotland in 1986 and the 14th will be in Auckland, New Zealand, in 1990.

　　　　On Commonwealth Day

　　*　Young visitors to Commonwealth Day activities (e.g. pupils'
　　　younger brothers and sisters) can be taught children's
　　　games from different Commonwealth countries.

　　*　Charts, drawings and written work on the Commonwealth Games
　　　can be exhibited.

　　*　The school could hold its own Commonwealth Games with
　　　pupils playing the part of athletes from different
　　　countries.

STAMPS

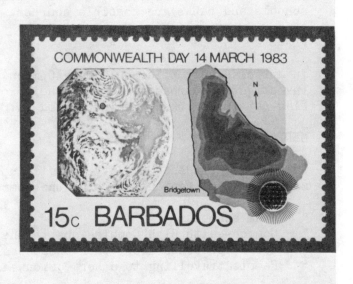

Commonwealth Day stamps.

STAMPS   **Level: Infant/junior/secondary**

Pupils can collect stamps from Commonwealth countries, including those sent by pen-friends, and make a display, grouping the stamps by region or by theme.

What can be learnt about the different countries by observing the subjects portrayed on the stamps?

Pupils may be able to find stamps issued for Commonwealth Day 1983.

They could design Commonwealth Day stamps for their own country, incorporating the Commonwealth symbol and illustrating something of importance either to the particular country or to the Commonwealth.

COINS   **Level: Infant/junior/secondary**

Pupils may be able to exhibit a collection of Commonwealth countries' coins. Pen friends, visitors from other Commonwealth countries, link schools and banks are possible sources.

FLAGS   **Level: Infant/junior/secondary**

In art classes pupils could make Commonwealth flags. They could investigate the reasons for the choice of designs and emblems. A flag-raising ceremony could be held on Commonwealth Day.

MEDIA   **Level: Top junior/secondary**

Teachers or students can try to build up a collection of newspapers and magazines from various parts of the Commonwealth. Possible sources are:

* Link schools
* Commonwealth High Commissions in the capital city
* Local residents from other Commonwealth countries
* People travelling to other Commonwealth countries

Students can go through the newspapers and identify events and concerns of particular importance to the country in question. They can cut out articles and photographs that interest them, paste them on posters and write short comments beside them. They can describe the impression they gain of the country by reading one of its national newspapers.

What references to other Commonwealth countries can be found in the foreign news sections? (National newspapers in the students' own country can be used in this way too.) What interaction between Commonwealth countries can be identified? Which are the problems that appear most often and what is the Commonwealth's attitude to these problems?

Radio and/or television can also be used as a source of information about the Commonwealth. Students can keep a record of relevant news items and discuss their significance in class. If the external services from countries like Britain, Australia and New Zealand operate in the locality it can be used as a source of information on the region and will also provide some insights into other parts of the world, particularly the Commonwealth.

Students could produce their own newspaper or magazine on Commonwealth affairs and events in member countries. They could write to the Commonwealth Secretariat in London for sample copies of Commonwealth Currents (see Section 10: Resources) and use these for further information and ideas.

Students could make their own 'radio programme' to include a summary of major Commonwealth news items, interviews with local residents from other Commonwealth countries, and interviews with prominent Commonwealth figures (these roles being played by students).

On Commonwealth Day

*   Display newspapers and magazines, including those made by the students.

*   Produce a live 'radio' or 'TV' show, using a 'phone-in' format or studio audience so that visitors to the school can participate too.

THE COMMONWEALTH PRESS

DAILY NEWS

). 4571 — PRICE: FOUR SHILLINGS, KENYA 4/-

TANZANIA

WEDNESDAY, OCTOBER 14, 1987.

Barbados Advocate

"Your National Newspaper"

The New Zealand Herald

elephones { Classified Advertising · 798-777
Other Departments · 795-050

AUCKLAND, FRIDAY, AUGUST 14, 1987

Price 40c — Air Freight 45c

THE GUARDIAN

Published in London and Manchester

Monday 26 October 1987   25p

THE HINDUSTAN TIMES

Regd.No. D-(c)167   Vol LXIV No. 292

Published from Delhi and Patna

New Delhi Tuesday October 20 1987

Late City   20 Pages   Rs 1.20

RELIGIONS

All the major world religions are practised in the Commonwealth. Students could find out which religions are practised in different Commonwealth countries and learn about the main beliefs and practices of each. Within the school or the class there may well be students of different religions, so knowledge can be shared among the students. Local residents may also be able to come and talk about the religions they practise and bring in holy books, artefacts etc. associated with these faiths.

On Commonwealth Day

The project could lead to a multi-faith observance on Commonwealth Day. Traditionally this consists of a procession of flags of Commonwealth countries (in the order determined by the date of membership of the Commonwealth); the national anthem and hymns; readings from Buddhist, Christian, Hindu, Islamic, Jewish and Sikh holy books; five affirmations of common faith; prayers from the different religions; and another procession as the flags are borne out.

From the Bhagavad Gita

He sees his soul as one with all beings, and all beings as one with his soul; his soul joined in union, beholding Oneness everywhere. Who sees Me everywhere, and sees all in Me, him I lose not, nor will he lose Me.

The knowledge whereby one eternal nature is perceived in all beings, undivided, though beings are divided, know that knowledge to be of Substance.

From the Metta Sutta (Loving-Kindness)

Whatever living beings there be - feeble or strong, long, stout or medium, short, small or large, seen or unseen, those dwelling far or near, those who are born and those who are to be born - may all beings, without exception, be happy-minded'

Let none deceive another nor despite any person whatever in any place. In anger or ill-will let him not wish any harm to another.

Just as a mother would protect her only child at the risk of her own life, even so, let him cultivate a boundless heart towards all beings.

From the Qur'an

All that is in heaven and earth gives glory to Allah. He is
the Mighty, the Wise One.

He is the first and the last, the visible and the unseen. He
has knowledge of all things.

He created the heavens and the earth in six days and then
mounted his Throne. He knows all that goes into the earth and
all that emerges from it, all that comes down from heaven and
all that ascends to it. He is with you wherever you are.
Allah is cognisant of all your actions.

From the Bible

What, then, does the Lord your God ask of you? Only to fear
the Lord your God, to conform to all his ways, to love him and
to serve him with all your heart and soul... The Lord secures
justice for widows and orphans, and loves the alien who lives
among you... You too must love the alien, for once you lived
as aliens.

Above all, keep your love for one another at full strength...
Whatever gift each of you may have received, use it in service
to one another.

5
SHARED PRINCIPLES

The Commonwealth symbol.

THE DECLARATION OF COMMONWEALTH PRINCIPLES

The Commonwealth of Nations is a voluntary association of independent sovereign states, each responsible for its own policies, consulting and co-operating in the common interests of their peoples and in the promotion of international understanding and world peace.

Members of the Commonwealth come from territories in the six continents and five oceans, include peoples of different races, languages and religions, and display every stage of economic development from poor developing nations to wealthy industrialised nations. They encompass a rich variety of cultures, traditions and institutions.

Membership of the Commonwealth is compatible with the freedom of member governments to be non-aligned or to belong to any other grouping, association or alliance. Within this diversity all members of the Commonwealth hold certain principles in common. It is by pursuing these principles that the Commonwealth can continue to influence international society for the benefit of mankind.

We believe that international peace and order are essential to the security and prosperity of mankind; we therefore support the United Nations and seek to strengthen its influence for peace in the world, and its efforts to remove the causes of tension between nations.

We believe in the liberty of the individual, in equal rights for all citizens regardless of race, colour, creed or political belief, and in their inalienable right to participate by means of free and democratic political processes in framing the society in which they live. We therefore strive to promote in each of our countries those representative institutions and guarantees for personal freedom under the law that are our common heritage.

We recognise racial prejudice as a dangerous sickness threatening the healthy development of the human race and racial discrimination as an unmitigated evil of society. Each of us will vigorously combat this evil within our own nation. No country will afford to regimes which practise racial discrimination assistance which in its own judgement directly contributes to the pursuit or consolidation of this evil policy.

We oppose all forms of colonial domination and racial oppression and are committed to the principles of human dignity and equality. We will therefore use all our efforts to foster human equality and dignity everywhere, and to further the principles of self-determination and non-racialism.

We believe that the wide disparities in wealth now existing between different sections of mankind are too great to be tolerated. They also create world tensions. Our aim is their progressive removal. We therefore seek to use our efforts to overcome poverty, ignorance and disease, in raising standards of life and achieving a more equitable international society.

To this end our aim is to achieve the freest possible flow of international trade on terms fair and equitable to all, taking into account the special requirements of the developing countries, and to encourage the flow of adequate resources, including governmental and private resources, to the developing countries, bearing in mind the importance of doing this in a true spirit of partnership and of establishing for this purpose in the developing countries conditions which are conducive to sustained investment and growth.

We believe that international co-operation is essential to remove the causes of war, promote tolerance, combat injustice, and secure development among the peoples of the world. We are convinced that the Commonwealth is one of the most fruitful associations for these purposes.

In pursuing these principles the members of the Commonwealth believe that they can provide a constructive example of the multi-national approach which is vital to peace and progress in the modern world. The association is based on consultation, discussion and co-operation.

In rejecting coercion as an instrument of policy they recognise that the security of each member state from external aggression is a matter of concern to all members. It provides many channels for continuing exchanges of knowledge and views on professional, cultural, economic, legal and political issues among member states.

These relationships we intend to foster and extend, for we believe that our multi-national association can expand human understanding and understanding among nations, assist in the elimination of discrimination based on differences of race, colour or creed, maintain and strengthen personal liberty, contribute to the enrichment of life for all, and provide a powerful influence for peace among nations.

SINGAPORE 1971

The activities in this section are designed to help students think about
some of the ideals expressed in the Declaration of Commonwealth Principles
of 1971 (pp. 39 and 40) and the problems that need to be tackled and
overcome.

Older students could do more detailed and searching work on the
Declaration of Commonwealth Principles and on the other Declarations and
Statements which have issued from subsequent Heads of Government
Meetings.   These include:

    The Gleneagles Agreement on Sporting Contacts with South Africa (1977)
    The Lusaka Declaration on Racism and Racial Prejudice (1979)
    The Melbourne Declaration (1981)
    The Goa Declaration on International Security (1983)
    The New Delhi Statement on Economic Action (1983)
    The Nassau Accord on Southern Africa (1985)
    The Okanagan Statement and Programme of Action on Southern Africa
    (1987)
    The Vancouver Declaration on World Trade (1987)

The four suggested activities relate to the following principles in the
1971 Declaration (see previous pages for full text):

**We believe that international peace and order are essential to the
security and prosperity of mankind.**

We recognise racial prejudice as a dangerous sickness.

**We believe that the wide disparities in wealth now existing between
different sections of mankind are too great to be tolerated.**

We believe that international co-operation is essential.

Activity 1: PRIORITIES FOR PEACE   **Level: Infant/junior/secondary**

(a) As a preliminary to the main activity, ask students to draw pictures
    or 'mental maps' illustrating their ideas about one of the following:

        Peace and conflict in our community

        Planet Earth (showing what is going well and what is going badly)

        A peaceful world

    Working in pairs or small groups, students should then talk about
    their pictures and discuss why they have chosen them.

(b) Next, ask students - still in their pairs or groups - to look at nine
    statements about peace (or, alternatively, war or conflict). These
    can be thought up by the students themselves, or a list such as the
    one below can be provided. **The nine statements are NOT statements of
    truth; they represent nine possible viewpoints and in some cases are
    deliberately provocative.** Each statement should be written on a
    separate card or piece of paper. Students select the ones they agree
    with and the ones they disagree with. They should discuss why they
    find certain ideas appealing or convincing and others unacceptable.
    Then they should rank the nine statements according to the priorities
    they agree upon as important. A diamond shape may be used as a way of
    allowing some ideas to be given equal importance.

Images of peace

"Rival superpowers having equal stockpiles of nuclear and conventional
weapons so that neither will risk attacking the other."

"A beautiful garden. Cool shade under the trees on a hot day. Birds
singing."

"A country run democratically, everyone having shelter, education and
medical care, everyone participating in developing."

"A group of children playing with toy weapons, everyone joining in."

"USA, USSR, Britain and France agreeing to stop supplying armaments to
other countries."

"Two friends arguing on a subject they both feel strongly about but
without losing their tempers."

"Someone near death at peace with the people they have known and with
God."

"A government succeeding in stamping out a group of terrorists who have
been planting bombs in shops and railway stations."

"Two countries trading with each other - one selling raw materials and the
other manufactured goods."

This activity could be followed by an examination of the Commonwealth's part in conflict-solving or working for peace and security e.g. its role in assisting Zimbabwe to gain independence; the concern for the security of small states, expressed in the Goa Declaration; support of the liberation of Namibia and South Africa. (See Section 10: Resources).

On Commonwealth Day

* Display 'mental maps' and pictures and 'priorities for peace' materials.

* Exhibit written and other work on Commonwealth conflict-solving activities.

Activity 2: LEARNING ABOUT DISCRIMINATION   Level:Junior/secondary

This activity is intended as a way into the question of racial discrimina-
ation but could also be applied to discrimination on the ground of gender
or religion.

The teacher selects one or more arbitrary factors about the children's
appearance or background and deliberately discriminates on the basis of
these:

e.g. all students above (or below) a certain height;
     all students who were born over 10 miles away;
     all students who are left-handed.

These students (group A) are asked to go and sit on one side of the classroom while the other (group B) move to the other side.

The teacher then describes a task that the whole class is to do. It
should be something that students generally enjoy doing, e.g. some kind of
art or craft work, and which requires the use of a number of materials.
Each member of group B is given plenty of materials - paper, several
coloured pencils, rulers, rubbers, scraps of cloth, scissors etc. - while
group A are given only a few basic things between them and do not have
enough to go round.

Half way through the activity the teacher distributes sweets, fruit or
cold drinks to group B and tells Group A to stand up for five minutes.
The class is then told to resume the activity.

At the end of the exercise the students should be encouraged to talk about
what went on and how they felt:

-   How did it feel to be discriminated against and was there any good
    reason for their being picked on?

-   How did it feel to be in the privileged group?

-   Was there any sharing of materials a) among group A? b) between the
    two groups?

-   Were some students separated from their friends and did they feel
    differently towards them when they were in a different group?

It is important at this stage that Group A is given its share of goodies,
previously distributed only to Group B, and that they are thanked for
putting up with the various examples of unfairness.

The activity can lead on to a discussion of racial (and other forms of)
discrimination in society.

The teacher might also like to introduce the subject of apartheid in South
Africa and Namibia and the Commonwealth's role in taking action against
apartheid:

e.g. Mission to South Africa: The Commonwealth Report of the Eminent
     Persons Group on Southern Africa (1986); the Gleneagles Agreement
     banning all sporting contacts with South Africa; the Nassau Accord on
     Southern Africa;

     the training of Namibians and black South Africans under the
     Secretariat's Fellowships and Training Scheme;

     distance-learning projects for South Africans and Namibians in
     refugee camps.

     (See Section 10: Resources).

The activities and discussion could lead on to written work and art work.

On Commonwealth Day

* Display essays, art work, charts on Commonwealth action
   against apartheid, and relevant Commonwealth declarations
   (e.g. Lusaka, Gleneagles)

* Make up a play about racial prejudice, based on the
   discrimination exercise above.

Activity 3: FAIR SHARES FOR ALL?   **Level: Secondary**

First ask the students to think about what is meant by 'wide disparities
in wealth'. What things do some people have in excess while other people
are denied even their basic needs? Ask for ideas from the students and
make a list on the blackboard. It could be divided into two columns to
show the extremes of wealth and poverty. Encourage the student to think
not just of property but also of rights, access to education, health,
political decision-making etc.

The list can then be used as a starting point for a discussion about the
reasons for such unequal distribution of wealth and power. What kinds of
people possess wealth? Who controls the economy? What causes poverty?
It is important to look both at inequalities in the students' own
societies and in the world generally. What connections are there between
the industrialised countries and the rich and powerful in developing
countries? What about the links and common ground between workers/
unemployment in 'developed countries' and those in the 'Third World'.

Explore the theme through role-play. Take, for example, the situation of
a country dependent on a single cash-crop such as sugar. A realistic
scenario could be that world sugar prices are falling and, because of
drought, the sugar crop is in danger of failing. The multi-national
companies may withdraw their investment in favour of European sugar beet.
Living and working conditions for the plantation workers are deterior-
ating. The Ministry of Economic Planning would like to diversify the
economy but the International Monetary Fund (IMF) will only supply the
loan needed for this project if the country agrees to devalue its
currency, a step it is reluctant to take because of the further hardship
that would be caused. Other factors can be added to the basic scenario
e.g. a women's organisation campaigning for fairer wages and better
conditions - the 'story' can be developed according to the students' own
ideas or experience. Students act the parts of plantation workers,
plantation owner, government officials etc. - either working out dialogues
between the various people, as appropriate, or being interviewed by
another group of students who play the part of 'journalists' covering the
story for national or regional newspapers. Afterwards it is important for
students to discuss how they felt in the roles they played and what they
have learnt about the causes of economic hardship.

As with the previous activities, there could be a follow-up study of the
Commonwealth's role in working towards a fairer world economy:

e.g. The New Delhi Statement on Economic Action;

    Secretary-General Shridath Ramphal's membership of the Brandt
    Commission;

The work of the Economic Affairs Division of the Commonwealth
Secretariat;

The preparing of reports on protectionism, debt, North-South dialogue
etc.

(See Resources, Section 10)

On Commonwealth Day

*   Develop the role-play exercise into a play to perform to
    the rest of the school and to visitors.

*   Hold a debate on inequalities within the Commonwealth (see
    Section 9 Facts and Figures)

This game places participants in a conflict situation which cannot end until each group co-operates.

1. Before class prepare a set of squares for each group of five children. (A set consists of five envelopes containing pieces of stiff paper cut into patterns that will form five 8cm x 8cm squares as below).

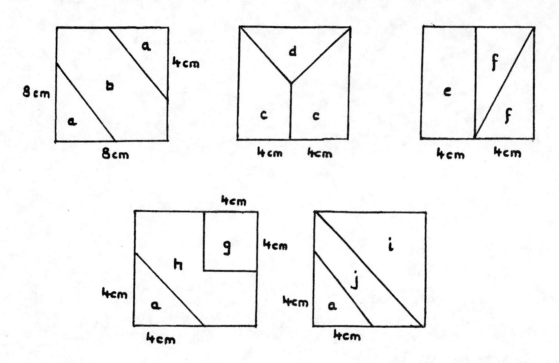

Several individual combinations will be possible but only one total combination.

2. Cut the squares into parts a to j and lightly pencil in the letters. Then mark the envelopes A to E and distribute the pieces thus: envelope A - pieces a, c, h, i; envelope B - pieces a, a, a, e; envelope C - piece j only; envelope D - pieces d and f; envelope E - pieces b, c, f, g. Erase the small letters from the pieces and write instead the envelope letters A to E so that the pieces can be easily returned for re-use.

3. Divide the class into groups of five and seat each group at a table. Give each group member an envelope and ask that the envelope be opened only on a signal.

4. Describe the game as a puzzle involving conflict and co-operation. Read the instructions aloud and give the signal to open the envelopes. The instructions are as follows:

> "Each person has an envelope containing pieces for forming squares. At the signal, the task of the group is to form five squares of equal size. The task is not completed until everyone has before him or her a perfect square, and all the squares are of the same size.
>
> During the game no member may speak. No member may communicate in any way - by smiles, hand-signals, longing glances etc. No member may take a puzzle piece from anyone else. Members may give puzzle pieces to others. Some class members should be observers. As groups finish allow them to observe other groups - silently."

5. It will usually take about 20 minutes for all groups to finish. You should spend at least as much time discussing the game as you spend playing it.

The following questions might be helpful in provoking discussion:

1. How did you feel?

2. How did the holder of envelope C feel?

3. Did anyone notice that C had only one piece?

4. How did you feel when someone held a piece and did not see the solution?

5. Why did you take all the pieces?

6. What was your reaction when someone finished a square and then sat back without seeing if that solution prevented others from solving the problem?

7. Were you afraid you would look foolish because you couldn't see a solution?

8. What were your feelings if you finished your square and then began to realise you would have to break it up and give away a piece?

9. How did you feel about a person who did not follow directions?

10. How did you feel about a person who was slow at seeing the solution or who misunderstood the instructions?

11. What processes enabled some groups to finish quickly? Did you follow the instructions? If not, how do you feel? Satisfied? Angry?

Obviously this game is geared to older children, but an enterprising teacher could adapt it for juniors.

After this activity the theme of co-operation can be looked at within the context of Commonwealth affairs. Co-operation on the political level is particularly relevant here (co-operation for development will be considered in some detail in Section 7) e.g. co-operative measures taken against South Africa following the Nassau summit.

6

A CHANGING ASSOCIATION
Commonwealth past,
present and future

Freedom Jump – Zimbabwe.

JOINING THE COMMONWEALTH

Country	Year of Membership	Country	Year of Membership
Antigua & Barbuda	1981	Malta	1964
Australia	*1931	Mauritius	1968
The Bahamas	1973	Nauru	1968
Bangladesh	1972	New Zealand	*1931
Barbados	1966	Nigeria	1960
Belize	1981	Papua New Guinea	1975
Botswana	1966	St Kitts and Nevis	1983
Britain		St Lucia	1979
Brunei Darussalam	1984	St Vincent & the	1979
Canada	*1931	Grenadines	
Cyprus	1961	Seychelles	1976
Dominica	1978	Sierra Leone	1961
The Gambia	1965	Singapore	1965
Ghana	1957	Solomon islands	1978
Grenada	1974	Sri Lanka	1948
Guyana	1966	Swaziland	1968
India	** 1947	Tanzania	1961
Jamaica	1962	Tonga	1970
Kenya	1963	Trinidad & Tobago	1962
Kiribati	1979	Tuvalu	1978
Lesotho	1966	Uganda	1962
Malawi	1964	Vanuatu	1980
Malaysia	1957	Western Samoa	1970
Maldives	1982	Zambia	1964
		Zimbabwe	1980

* Independence from Britain obtained under the Statute of Westminster

** India became a republic but asked to become a member of the Commonwealth accepting the British monarch as head of the Commonwealth

The cultural diversity of the Commonwealth is a valuable area of study but does not of itself clarify the concept of the Commonwealth as an entity. After all, studies of non-Commonwealth countries, including projects on food, clothes, customs etc., would have a similar effect of raising students' awareness of cultures other than their own. Equally, the notion of shared principles, though an important binding force in the Commonwealth, is not exclusive to the Commonwealth. It underlies other international and regional organisations too.

So it is important that students learn about the specificities of the Commonwealth too. The activities in this section are designed to raise awareness of Commonwealth history and evolution, and those in the next section explore some of the ways in which the Commonwealth is operating in the world today.

Activity 1: COMMONWEALTH HISTORY IN MAPS   **Level: Junior/secondary**

Listed on page 53 are all 48 members of the Commonwealth with the date on which they became independent and, in turn, voluntarily, became members of the Commonwealth:

On a blank map of the world (p.55):

a   Colour in blue all the countries which were full members of the Commonwealth in 1931.

b   Now add, in green all the countries which joined between 1932 and 1949.

c   Finally colour in yellow all the countries which have joined the Commonwealth between 1950 and 1987.

Briefly describe the changes in the membership of the Commonwealth. Who were the founder members? During which decade did membership of the Commonwealth grow most rapidly?

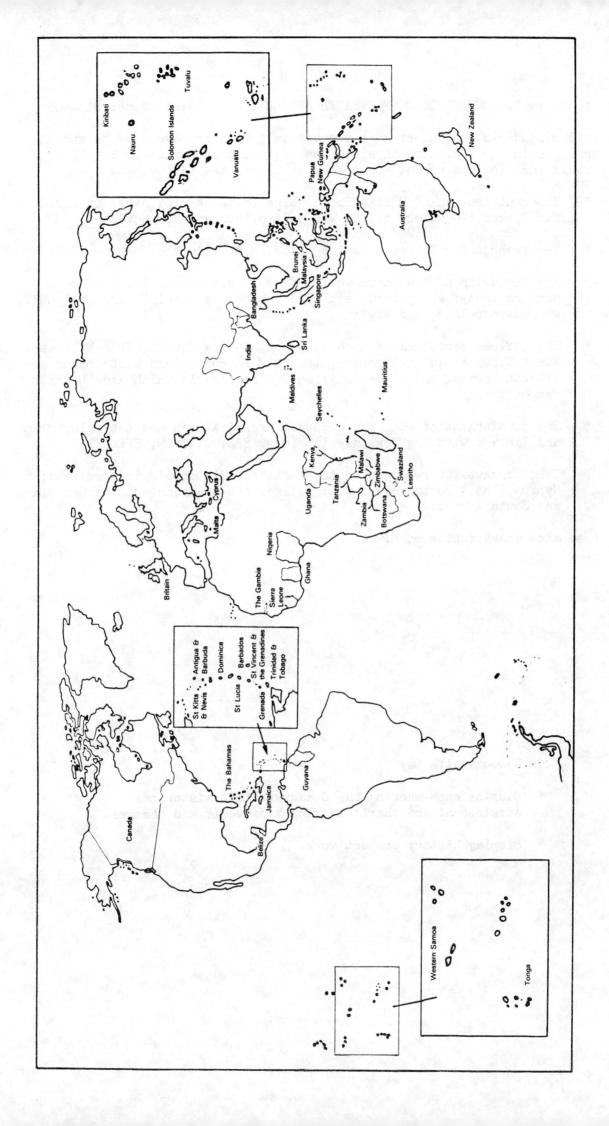

Activity 2: PROJECT ON COMMONWEALTH HISTORY   Level: Upper secondary

Older students can undertake a project on the major developments and changes in the Commonwealth since the beginning of World War 2. This could include finding out about some or all of the following:

*   The contribution of Britain's colonies to the Allied cause in World War 2, and the effect of the war on the independence movement;

*   The reasons for former colonies choosing to join the Commonwealth;

*   The expansion of the Commonwealth from 10 members in 1957 to 48 members today: who joined, and why?; who did not join?; who resigned?; who was expelled, and why?;

*   The influence of leaders such as Nehru, Indira Gandhi, Eric Williams, Kwame Nkrumah, Julius Nyerere, Lester B Pearson, John Diefenbaker and Kenneth Kaunda, and of Secretaries-General Arnold Smith and Shridath Ramphal;

*   The development of regional economic organisations and their impact on and linkage with the Commonwealth (e.g. EEC, CARICOM, SPEC);

*   The Commonwealth response to the fight for Zimbabwe's independence; Cyprus; the Nigerian civil war; Belize; the Grenadan crisis; Namibia and South Africa.

See also essay topics on p.96.

On Commonwealth Day

*   **Display maps showing the Commonwealth's historical development and charts listing key events and changes.**

*   **Display history project work.**

7
WORKING TOGETHER

MAJOR OUTCOMES OF RECENT HEADS OF GOVERNMENT MEETINGS

* **1961:** The cardinal principal of racial equality was reaffirmed. South Africa was obliged to withdraw its application to remain a member of the Commonwealth after becoming a republic.

* **1965:** Heads of Government agreed to set up the Commonwealth Secretariat.

* **1966 Lagos:** First meeting held outside Britain, convened to formulate a Commonwealth response to Rhodesia declaring a Unilateral Declaration of Independence.

* **1966 London:** Britain agreed to Heads of Governments' request that Rhodesia would not be granted independence without majority rule.

* **1971 Singapore:** The Declaration of Commonwealth Principles was issued. The Commonwealth Fund for Technical Co-operation was established.

* **1977 London:** Rhodesia and South Africa were high on the agenda. The Gleneagles Agreement was issued, stating the Commonwealth's opposition to sporting links with South Africa.

* **1979 Lusaka:** Heads of Government issued the Lusaka Declaration on Racism and Racial Prejudice. Heads of Government persuaded Britain that settlement of the Rhodesian crisis could not be achieved without the participation of the Patriotic Front, and the way was paved for the Lancaster House talks which led to the independence of Zimbabwe. It was agreed that the Commonwealth would send a team of observers to supervise elections of a new government in Zimbabwe. The Commonwealth Secretariat's Industrial Development Unit was established.

* **1983 New Delhi:** The nuclear arms build-up and the fragility of international security led to Heads of Government issuing the Goa Declaration on International Security. Commonwealth commitment to a New International Economic Order was reaffirmed in the New Delhi Statement on Economic Action.

* **1985 Nassau:** The meeting was dominated by the problem of South Africa and sanctions against South Africa. In the Nassau Accord on Southern Africa a number of 'measures' were agreed upon. Heads of Government set up a Group of Eminent Persons charged with encouraging political dialogue in South Africa with a view to establishing a non-racial and representative government.

* **1987 Vancouver:** The Okanagan Statement and Programme of Action on Southern Africa reaffirmed the shared international responsibility for the total eradication of apartheid. The Vancouver Declaration on World Trade underlined the need for a more open, viable and durable multilateral trading system to promote growth and development. Fiji's membership of the Commonwealth lapsed with the declaration of the Republic. Agreement was reached on the creation of a Commonwealth institution to promote co-operation in distance education.

This section is concerned with the question of how the Commonwealth 'works' today: how the Commonwealth Secretariat and the Commonwealth Fund for Technical Co-operation (CFTC) operate, and what kinds of development projects both the 'official' and the 'unofficial' Commonwealth are involved in. It takes the form of information followed by suggested activities, the purpose of which is to translate the various types of work and co-operation to a local level, within the school and the community. These small-scale co-operative or development projects are not specifically Commonwealth activities but are designed to give practical expression to the aims and principles underlying the work of Commonwealth organisations.

COMMONWEALTH HEADS OF GOVERNMENT MEETINGS

Commonwealth summits attended by Heads of Government - Presidents or Prime Ministers, or their representatives - take place every two years. For a full week intensive discussions are held on matters of concern to the Commonwealth - both global affairs and intra-Commonwealth affairs - and the meetings are characterised by an atmosphere of informality. Plans for future Commonwealth action are laid and at the end of the meeting a communique is issued: this consists of a statement of decisions and views which have been reached by consensus. The meetings are held in different Commonwealth capitals. Some of the more important outcomes of recent meetings are listed on p.58.

Activity 1: WORKING TOWARDS CONSENSUS   **Level: Upper secondary**

This activity allows students to state their views on a subject, to examine each others' views critically but positively, to indicate their agreements and disagreements, and to reach a consensus. It is intended as a preparation for the mock Heads of Government meeting (Activity 2, p.61)

Students form small groups of five or six. Each person is given four cards or slips of paper. On each of these he or she is to write a contribution to a group statement on the subject-matter under consideration. The subject should be one on which the students will have views of their own; in the example here 'education' is chosen as the topic. (see p. 60).

When each student has written four statements, one on each of the four cards or slips of paper, the statements are collected in, and shuffled as in a game of cards. They are then dealt out - three for each 'player', with the rest placed face upwards on the table.

Everyone looks at his or her hand. They should discard anything which they wrote themselves, and anything they disagree with. From the 'pool' they select cards with which they agree, provided they have not written them themselves. The students continue to discard and pick up until they have three (or four) cards with which they agree.

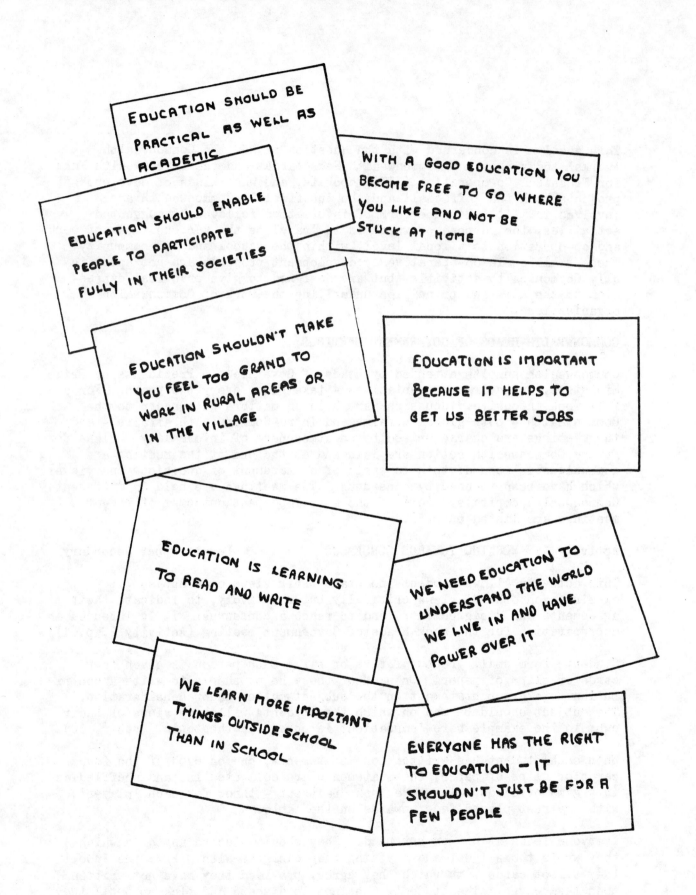

EDUCATION SHOULD BE PRACTICAL AS WELL AS ACADEMIC

EDUCATION SHOULD ENABLE PEOPLE TO PARTICIPATE FULLY IN THEIR SOCIETIES

WITH A GOOD EDUCATION YOU BECOME FREE TO GO WHERE YOU LIKE AND NOT BE STUCK AT HOME

EDUCATION SHOULDN'T MAKE YOU FEEL TOO GRAND TO WORK IN RURAL AREAS OR IN THE VILLAGE

EDUCATION IS IMPORTANT BECAUSE IT HELPS TO GET US BETTER JOBS

EDUCATION IS LEARNING TO READ AND WRITE

WE NEED EDUCATION TO UNDERSTAND THE WORLD WE LIVE IN AND HAVE POWER OVER IT

WE LEARN MORE IMPORTANT THINGS OUTSIDE SCHOOL THAN IN SCHOOL

EVERYONE HAS THE RIGHT TO EDUCATION — IT SHOULDN'T JUST BE FOR A FEW PEOPLE

Groups sub-divide into twos and threes to discuss the statements selected and to make a composite statement. Then the group comes together as a whole, discusses the different viewpoints and arrives at a consensus. After the exercise it is important that the class analyses the process of reaching a consensus.

Variation

If it is feared that any one student's ideas may be completely rejected by all the others, the game can be adapted so that each participant is to have a final hand of four cards, at least two of which were written by someone else.

Actity 2: A STUDENT 'HEADS OF GOVERNMENT' MEETING   Level: Secondary

Senior secondary students should find the holding of a mock Heads of Government meeting an enjoyable and valuable exercise. First they should be briefed on the informal procedure of these meetings. Then they should decide on one or more topics of international importance to be discussed at the meeting.

One student acts the part of Commonwealth Secretary-General; the others are Heads of Government. They should not prepare formal speeches but may, if they wish, circulate prepared texts before the meeting. They certainly need to do some 'homework' on the topic, or at least some careful thinking beforehand, if the discussion is to be worthwhile.

At the meeting itself 'Heads of Government' sit in a circle. The meeting is chaired by the Head of State of the host country.

Interventions should be short and succinct. Nobody should be allowed to 'hold the floor'. Any decisions made should be reached by consensus; at the end of the meeting a communique should be issued, stating the Commonwealth's position on the world issue(s) discussed.

Activity 3: A HEADS OF GOVERNMENT 'PRESENTATION'   Level: Junior

For younger children Heads of Government meetings could be represented in a simple dramatic performance. The pupils could each represent a head of government (or a country), walk across the stage bearing that country's flag, and announce the country and president or prime minister they represent. They could also prepare posters listing dates and venues of Heads of Government meetings.

THE COMMONWEALTH SECRETARIAT

The main agency through which Commonwealth countries work together is the Commonwealth Secretariat, established by Heads of Government in 1965. The Secretariat organises consultations between governments, services Commonwealth meetings, conducts programmes of co-operation and is a central source of information. It is funded by all member governments in varying proportions and works under their overall direction.

The Secretariat is active in many different fields, as shown in the diagram below; departments work together as much as possible, so that they can benefit from each other's expertise. Heading the Secretariat is the Commonwealth Secretary-General, elected by Heads of Government; there are two Deputy Secretaries-General, also elected by governments, one responsible for political affairs and the other for economic affairs; all other staff are appointed by the Secretary-General and in 1987 numbered 419 people from 30 different countries. The current Secretary-General, Shridath Ramphal, former Minister of Foreign Affairs and Justice of Guyana, was re-elected to a third five-year term from July 1985.

The Secretariat also includes the Commonwealth Fund for Technical Co-operation (CFTC) which is the Commonwealth's own multilateral agency. It provides technical assistance to all developing countries by injecting expertise through 300 long- and short-term experts each year. The CFTC also funds training awards and fellowships, assists the expansion of industry and exports and offers a consultancy service on a wide range of development concerns.

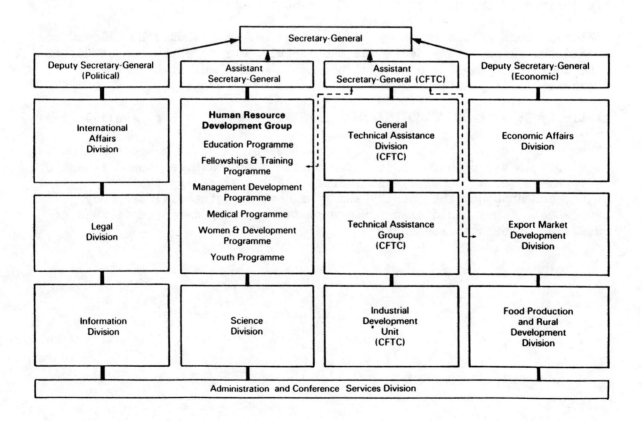

Activity 1: LOOKING AT THE WORK OF THE COMMONWEALTH SECRETARIAT
                                                                    Level: Junior

Junior pupils could be given a simplified introduction to the work of the
Secretariat. They could prepare charts illustrating the Secretariat's
areas of work (see p.62). They could discuss why development work is
important in such areas as health, education, industry etc., looking
particularly at the needs of their own community. The Secretariat's role
in helping governments plan and carry out improvements could then be
explained in simple terms.

Some of the activities of the Secretariat and of non-governmental
Commonwealth organisations are referred to in more detail in the rest of
this section.

On Commonwealth Day

* **Display project work**

* **Juniors could put on a 'presentation' of the work of the
   Secretariat, using placards or banners on which its areas
   of work are printed and making short statements about
   each.**

WORKING FOR BETTER HEALTH

Commonwealth countries work together to improve health care. Here are some examples of their work:

* Health Ministers meet every three years to identify priorities for action.

* Workshops on health planning and management are run by the Secretariat and funded by the CFTC (Commonwealth Fund for Technical Co-operation).

* The training of nurses and other health workers is helped by CFTC's Fellowships and Training programme.

* Countries in the same region share training facilities - Regional Health Secretariats.

* Community health education is promoted through workshops and special surveys.

* The Commonwealth Nurses Federation puts nurses in different countries in touch with each other.

* The Royal Commonwealth Society for the Blind runs the world's largest sight restoration programme.

* Many other charitable organisations work with the deaf, children in need, the disabled, victims of leprosy, the handicapped and the elderly.

Activity 1: HEALTH SCOUTS   **Level: Junior/secondary**

Finding out about the health services available to the community

Often there are many people in the community with different kinds of health knowledge:

* People who know how to make herbal remedies
* Women who help at childbirth
* People who know about first aid
* Trained health workers in hospitals and clinics

Children can find out about the people in their community with some special health knowledge:

* Where they can be found
* What their special knowledge is

Discuss these things with the children and let them make a list of the people, e.g. clinic sister, midwife, herbalist.

Ask the children to make a health services map of their community (see p.65). On it they can mark where to go for help. Circles can be drawn to represent each hour's walk from home.

HEALTH ACTIVITIES

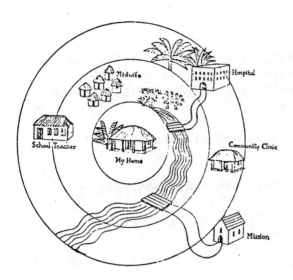

Health Map for our Village

OUR COMMUNITY - MAKING IT HEALTHIER

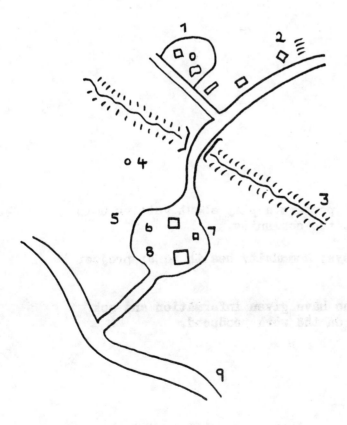

1 My House
   Prevent Accidents

2 Market
   Keep Clean

3 Stream
   Clear Snails

4 Well
   Fence Off

5 High Grass
   Cut Down

6 School
   Sweep Classrooms

7 Kitchen
   Kill Flies

8 School Garden
   Grow Vegetables

9 Main Road
   Safety Drill

The children could play games using their maps and asking each other, for instance, "If somebody gets burnt by the cooking fire, who will you get to help and how long will it take?"

Helping to care for the health of others

There are many ways in which children can help in looking after the health of others. For example, they can become helpers at the health clinic (see p.65). Teachers and health workers would need to plan this together, but some ways in which children can help are:

* Weighing babies, measuring arm circumference and filling in growth charts;

* Organising play groups for children waiting with their mothers;

* Acting as interpreters for mothers and health workers, to pass on instructions for feeding programmes or treatment;

* Helping to cook at feeding demonstrations;

* Helping to clean up at the clinic.

Carrying out an immunisation survey

Children can find out whether babies and young children have been immunised against diseases like tuberculosis, diptheria, whooping cough, tetanus, poliomyelitis and measles. They can assist health personnel collect these health statistics as well as spreading the message about immunisation clinics.

On Commonwealth Day

* Children can make up and perform a play about getting help from different people in the community.

* Display results of surveys; community health maps; project work.

* Invite all the people who have given information and ask them for their comments on the work produced.

MAKING THE COMMUNITY HEALTHIER

Talking about posters

A 'council' meeting

Activity 2: OUR COMMUNITY - MAKING IT HEALTHIER Level: Junior/secondary

The activities below are based on the idea that a community can become healthier:

* When the people in it understand better what their problems are and how they are caused;

* When the people communicate with one another and discuss what they can do to make their lives better;

* When they act to improve community health.

Children are important members of the community and can play a part in making a better neighbourhood. These activities are designed to:

* Encourage children to find out the factors which contribute to health or disease;

* Encourage children to think about how the community can help its children;

* Lead older children to think about actions they themselves can take to improve matters;

* Help children find ways of passing these ideas on to younger children.

Mapping the community

This could be done using copies of maps already prepared, or children could make their own maps. They need first to discuss what should be shown on the map (see p.65), e.g. they could identify:

* Areas where animals and insects spread diseases;

* Areas where accidents could easily happen;

* Areas where people spread diseases.

In some schools, and with younger children, it will be difficult to make a map of the neighbourhood; instead they can make a plan or a picture map of:

* Their home

* The school

* The way to school

Deciding what can be done

Children could look at their map and talk about what they have found. They need time to discuss what can be done and by whom. They may decide that action should be taken by different groups within the community.

Children themselves could tell other children in the school about their work. They could try to make their school a healthier place. They could talk with their parents about how improvements have been made in the past. They could talk with teachers about what the school could do.

Community action can be explored. Role play and drama can help the children understand how communities make decisions. Children can play the parts of council members, policemen, health aides, agricultural officers, elders and teachers. They could hold a simulated council meeting to discuss village and health problems (p.67).

Children could spread ideas to their friends and families. Teachers could remind them that sharing expertise is also an important part of the way the Commonwealth works.

Children could organise action campaigns and games e.g. "A clean school compound".

Other activities

Understanding and communication can be improved by various activities. Older children could become involved in:

*   Writing books or reading cards for younger children;

*   Drawing posters and helping younger ones to talk about them;

*   Designing health games to play with younger children;

*   Making plays and puppet shows for younger children;

*   Organising small children into teams to compete in cleaning up activities.

On Commonwealth Day

*   **Children's work - maps, posters, reading cards, drawings etc. - can be displayed.**

*   **Children can give a performance of the 'council' meeting to discuss community health problems and plans for action.**

*   **A local health worker who has been involved in the action campaign can be invited to speak about progress made and future plans.**

Activity 3: PRODUCING HEALTHY FOOD   **Level: Junior/secondary**

Children could discuss what kinds of food are needed for healthy growing
and which are the high energy foods.

Children set up their own food 'market'. They could make play money to
buy food for the family. They could plan the cheapest healthy menu. They
could visit the local market to observe prices of foods there.

Children could plan and cook healthy meals at school. Parents could be
invited to help teach the children.

Young children could be encouraged to plant a quick-growing vegetable
plant or fruit tree, e.g. tomato, in a pot. They could watch it grow and
then plant it in their garden at home.

Each class could plant vegetables and fruit trees in the schoolyard. The
produce could be taken home or used in school meals.

Each class in the school could measure the height and weight of everyone
in the class. Grades 5 and 6 could also help to measure the younger
children. All these measurements should be written up on a poster on the
wall. This activity can be carried out every 3 months and the results
compared.

Children could take their younger brothers and sisters who are under five
to be weighed each month.

On Commonwealth Day

* Work in progress and result of project can be displayed

Activity 4: PROJECTS FOR OLDER STUDENTS   **Level: Upper secondary**

Older students could try to find out about the drugs policy of their
country. They could find out about drugs imported from other Commonwealth
countries and what codes of practice the exporting country has to abide
by.

A mock meeting of Commonwealth health ministers could be organised. If
possible, students should do some research on what has happened at
previous meetings. The discussion can concentrate on identifying
priorities for action to be taken by Commonwealth countries, e.g. how to
prevent drugs trafficking; how to dissuade young people from experimenting
with drugs.

EDUCATION FOR DEVELOPMENT

Education is an important area of Commonwealth co-operation, assisted by the broad similarity of educational systems in member states. Many different activities are undertaken:

* Commonwealth Ministers of Education meet every three years to discuss what practical measures need to be taken.

* The CFTC provides educational advisers to governments and institutions.

* The Fellowships and Training Programme and the Commonwealth Scholarship and Fellowship Plan enable men and women to study or train in other Commonwealth countries.

* The Education Programme of the Commonwealth Secretariat holds conferences, workshops and training courses.

* Educational activities are often supported by the Commonwealth Foundation.

* Distance-education schemes have been set up for Namibian and South African refugees (see p.72).

Many non-governmental organisations are involved in education too. Among these are:-

* The Association of Commonwealth Universities which promotes, in practical ways, contact and co-operation between the universities of the Commonwealth;

* The Commonwealth Association of Polytechnics in Africa which operates on a regional basis.

* The Commonwealth Association of Science, Mathematics and Technology Educators (CASMTE).

* The Commonwealth Council for Educational Administration (CCEA).

* The Commonwealth Association for the Education and Training of Adults (CAETA).

DISTANCE EDUCATION FOR SOUTHERN AFRICA

Namibian artist's illustrations for teaching materials produced by the Commonwealth Secretariat and the South West African People's Organisation (SWAPO) for the Namibian Extension Unit.

EDUCATION

Namibians leave for India under CFTC's Namibian training programme.

Activity 1: CREATING A SCHOOL INFORMATION BASE   Level: Junior/secondary

The idea behind this activity is that every community has resources which can usefully be pooled and shared. Collecting the information will also require certain skills and attitudes that are considered essential by the Commonwealth: communication skills, respect for people of different kinds or performing different roles in society, and commitment to co-operation.

There are many possible sources of information:

    libraries
    post offices
    churches
    local and overseas organisations working locally (e.g. Christian
      Aid, Royal Commonwealth Society for the Blind)
    hospitals and clinics
    missions
    parents, teachers, students and other individuals
    train or bus stations, lorry parks
    police stations

In large towns or cities or in developed countries there are likely to be many more sources: community advice services, societies for special interests or voluntary work, museums, art galleries, travel agents, etc.

Overseas students can write to the Information Division of the Commonwealth Secretariat for help (see p.103).

The students should discuss what kinds of information material they are seeking. Where appropriate they should make appointments to go and see people who may be able to help them. They should explain what they are trying to do. If the school has its own library the school librarian will be a key resource person.

They will need to discuss where in the school the information base could be situated. Will extra shelving be needed? Who could help make this?

Could local shopkeepers provide boxes which could be used to divide the material into various categories?

The students can divide the material into subject areas, e.g. health services, local history, women's organisations, etc.

Remember that much of the information about the community will not be in written form. If tape-recorders are available students can gather a great deal of information by interviewing people (they should practice this on each other in the classroom first); if there are no tape-recorders students should take notes during interviews and write them up afterwards as information sheets or documents. Again, if cameras are available, photographs will greatly enrich the information base. Drawings and paintings may also be made.

   On Commonwealth Day

   * **Arrange a special opening of the information base. Invite
      one or more of the people who have provided information to
      officiate at the formal opening. Invite all the people who
      have co-operated to make the project possible.**

Activity 2: SHARING SKILLS AND KNOWLEDGE   Level: Infant/junior/secondary

Sharing expertise is a central principle of Commonwealth co-operation. Through its General Technical Assistance programme, the Commonwealth Fund for Technical Co-operation (CFTC) supplies experts, mainly from developing countries, to work in various development fields as requested by Commonwealth governments. Training programmes are seen as very important, as is regional co-operation.

Much can be shared in the school and in the community. As a pre-Commonwealth Day project a school could devise ways of sharing skills and knowledge. Starting off in the classroom, students can be asked:

- what they would like to learn that someone else in the class might be able to teach them;

- what skills or knowledge they have to pass on to others.

Examples could be first aid, speaking another language, a handicraft skill, cooking a special dish etc. Girls could teach boys some skills or domestic tasks which are conventionally the province of girls alone; boys could teach girls skills they do not normally have the opportunity to acquire. Over a number of weeks students can become involved in teaching or learning new skills, or both. Obviously the teacher must ensure a structure and support for this project.

A more ambitious project is for the school to share skills with the outside community. This should only be done after very careful consultation with the headteacher, governors, parents associations and local community groups.

On Commonwealth Day

* **Display of work/performances by those who have acquired new knowledge and skills.**

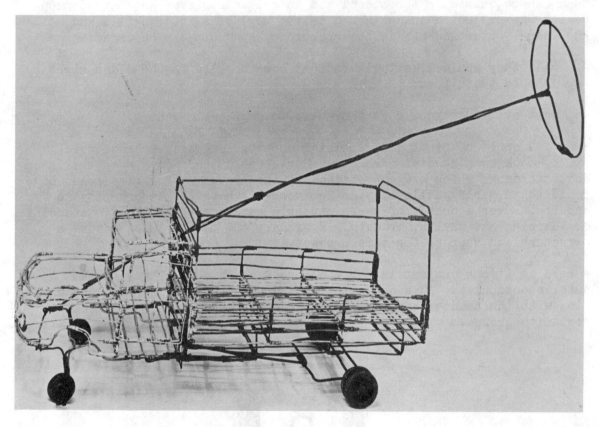

Wire trolley made by children.

Activity 3: MAKING TOYS AND GAMES FOR YOUNG CHILDREN

Level: Junior/secondary

Teachers can discuss with older children (say top junior upwards) why children need to play. (They learn mental, social, creative and physical skills through activities they enjoy).

Children can then talk together about the different toys they could make for their younger brothers and sisters or other small children, and where they should go to collect materials. There are many different sources in the community:

from shops	at home
scraps of cloth, packing material, cartons, bottle tops, etc.	tins, boxes, gourds, old or broken toy parts, etc.
from local craftspeople	from fields, forest, beaches
scraps of wood, metal, leather etc.	cornstalks, stones, shells, cloth, clay, sand, grasses, seed pods, leaves, etc.

Older children must be reminded to make sure that toys for young children are safe to use. They must avoid using:

- things with sharp edges;
- small pieces which young children can swallow or put up their noses;
- plastic bags, which can cause suffocation.

Different lessons can be used for making play materials.

The art and craft lesson	Toys, e.g. cars, lorries, dolls, models. Games equipment e.g. balls, hoops, ropes. Puppets Building blocks.
The language lesson	Books with stories and pictures. Reading cards with pictures and words. Posters and charts.
The maths or science lesson	Puzzles, shapes and dominoes. Games e.g. Snakes and Ladders.
The music lesson	Instruments, drums, rattles and flutes. Collections of songs and singing games for children to sing and play.

Other people may be able to help:

Craftspeople and parents may be needed occasionally to provide skills and labour.

Teachers may need to help children raise money for some materials.

Headteachers may be needed to arrange for the school to be used for playgroups.

Local women's groups or health workers may be needed to explain why children need to play.

WOMEN AND DEVELOPMENT

Indian woman uses tube well.

WOMEN AND DEVELOPMENT

The Women and Development Programme of the Secretariat, established in 1980 works to advance the interests of women in Commonwealth countries. It assists governments to help meet the needs of women and also helps women themselves to be more effective in advancing their own interests. Work undertaken so far includes:

* Organising a programme of training workshops to help women in responsible positions develop skills in organisation and communication.

* Assisting in the training of trainers in their awareness of the realities of women's contribution to society and the economy, so that women are properly integrated in development planning.

* Working with other divisions of the Secretariat to focus on women's activities.

* Helping governments to increase women's access to paid employment and income-earning projects.

* Research (undertaken by women themselves) on women's roles as good producers; time spent by women on fuel and water collection, harvesting, processing and storage of food; their access to extension services and credit.

* Promoting literacy and non-formal education projects for women.

* Working with the Secretariat's Health Programme to help alert mothers to the dangers of using infant food formulas (dried milk, etc.) with impure water.

* Circulating information on activities and policy changes relating to violence against women.

* Researching and carrying out surveys on women's activities in the informal sector.

* Collecting and distributing information about women in the Commonwealth (see Resources, Section 10).

Activity 1: A SCHOOL SURVEY ON ATTITUDES TO WOMEN AND NEEDS OF WOMEN
Level: Secondary

If the school is co-educational, girls should take the lead in devising the questionnaire and carrying out the survey. Questions should be designed to elicit answers revealing attitudes towards the status and role of women: the work they should/could do, their role in domestic life, child-rearing etc., their health and leisure needs, their part in national development, their right to gainful employment and control over their incomes. It should also seek to identify what women (and girls) need and want in terms of skills and resources to enable them to fully participate in society. It may be helpful to apply the questions to areas such as health, education, employment, agriculture, the family, politics etc.

Sample Questions:

	Men	Women	Both
Who are responsible for the following jobs and activities:			
cleaning the house			
gardening			
running the government			
looking after children			
cooking meals			
running factories			

	Men	Women	Both
Who should control how money is spent in families?			
How many hours of leisure/relaxation do people need per day?			

The results of the survey can then be analysed and discussed. Students can identify where attitudes need to be changed and where more provision for women/girls is needed.

They may want to put forward proposals for changes in the curriculum e.g. the introduction of vocational skills, management skills, book-keeping and learning about labour-saving technology, access to credit, land ownership, etc. They could also consider which of these new areas of learning could be undertaken in primary schools.

Activity 2: EXAMINING MEDIA IMAGES OF WOMEN AND MEN
Level: Top Junior/secondary

Teachers can encourage discussion, in groups, of popular television programmes, magazines, comics and newspapers, with a view to analysing how male and female characters are portrayed (e.g. clever/stupid, confident/ shy) to see whether gender stereotyping emerges. They may be able to acquire a few publications from other Commonwealth countries and see whether a similar pattern emerges in these. The students should then discuss in what way the media images may be inadequate, untrue, offensive etc. What changes would they like to see in the media's attitudes: What action can they take themselves?

Activity 3: FINDING OUT ABOUT WOMEN'S NEEDS IN THE COMMUNITY
Level: Secondary

Again this is an activity where girls can take a leading part.

Students could make contact with local women's organisations and find out what they see as the major problems faced by women and the main priorities for action.

How much time do women spend carrying water and firewood?

What problems do they face in agricultural work - weeding, sowing, planting, watering and harvesting?

Are they able to earn an income?

Are they being by-passed by local development projects?

Are they being included on training schemes e.g. learning new technology?

What about access to credit?

Do they have access to literacy schemes/continuing education?

After discussing the information they have gained, they could try to identify ways in which they may be able to help women in the community.

Could they assist with literacy teaching?
Could they share some of the skills they learn in school but which their mothers or other older women in the community may not have had the opportunity to learn?

Could they (boys and girls) help provide labour in bringing clean fresh water to the village?
Could they help maintain waterpoints?

Could they devise ways in which women can save labour and energy when carrying out agricultural or domestic tasks?

On Commonwealth Day

*   Questionnaires, charts, results of surveys etc. can be
    exhibited.

*   Women whom students have worked with can be invited to take
    part in celebrations, to contribute their ideas and skills.

*   An open discussion could be help on possibilities for
    further action benefiting women.

A windpump in Africa.

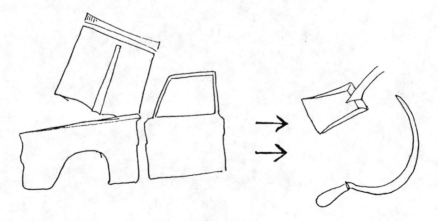

Scrap metal from cars used to make tools.

ACTION FOR INDUSTRY

The Industrial Development Unit (IDU) is part of the Commonwealth Fund for Technical Co-operation in the Commonwealth Secretariat. The IDU provides expertise to generate new industries or reactivate old ones:

e.g. * Electronic equipment for Trinidad and Tobago's sugar industry

* Manufacture of edible oil in Tuvalu, Kiribati and the Solomon Islands

* Solar salt projects in several Commonwealth countries.

* Ceramic industries in Guyana and Uganda

* Meat by-products in Uganda

It helps develop new uses for local resources:

e.g. * Glass-making in The Gambia, Ghana and Fiji

* Graphite in Sri Lanka

* Cement and concrete in Vanuatu

Farm-tools from scrap metal for SADCC countries

In Botswana, Lesotho and Tanzania, three of the countries linked through the Southern African Development Co-ordination Conference (SADCC), the IDU has helped set up hand-tool manufacturing units. Technicians from India, where blacksmithing skills are traditional, are helping the people make tools from scrap metal. They are now making:

axes	forks
hoes	shovels
sickles	slashers

Activity: RE-CYCLING MATERIAL   **Level: Top Junior/secondary**

Students could collect scrap metal, waste materials, discarded machine parts and broken furniture and try out ways of recycling them for new uses. If metalwork, woodwork or technical drawing classes are run in the school, projects could take place within these lessons and under the guidance of the teachers responsible.

If students make a careful study of their local environment, including their homes, it may be possible to identify areas of work where a simple gadget, tool, container etc. would make a task less arduous. In farming, for example, women are often not consulted when new machinery is introduced and it is important to find out from them what their needs are.

TRADING

The gourd seller.

PROMOTING EXPORTS

The CFTC assists member countries in increasing their earnings from exports. Its Export Market Development Division carries out market surveys, provides experts in marketing, puts on training courses in export sales techniques and organises 'buyer-seller meets'.

Activity 1: ORGANISE A MOCK 'BUYER-SELLER MEET'   Level: Secondary

Students play the parts of buyers from one country or sellers from another. It may be easier for students to relate to the activity if the country doing the selling (or, where appropriate, the one doing the buying) is their own. The students decide what products are to be promoted, which country is likely to be interested in buying, whether the products need to be adapted to meet the requirements of the export market, and how they should be packaged and presented. Advertising brochures can be prepared. An exhibition of products should be attractively mounted for the buyer-seller meet. Sellers explain the qualities and advantages of their products and try to persuade buyers to place orders; buyers ask questions about the products and put forward their views of what will sell well in their country.

On Commonwealth Day

*   **A buyer-seller meet could be enacted before an audience. The various stages before the meet takes place, and involving the expertise of the Export Marketing Division, could be shown as a series of very short scenes. At the buyer-seller meet itself the general hubbub and activity of trading can be 'frozen' at intervals: while everyone else remains silent and motionless two traders engage in a conversation; the general activity resumes, followed by another 'focus' on a different buyer and seller, etc.**

Activity 2: MARKET TRADING   Level: Infant/junior/secondary

(adapted according to age)

Children can be given an experience of trading and promoting products by running their own miniature market. Each brings one or more items from home, or makes an item e.g. in woodwork or home economics classes. Toy money could be used with young children, or if real currency is used the money raised could be donated to a local development project of the children's choice.

Teachers could consider ways in which this activity could be designed to increase understanding of the idea (inherent in the buyer-seller meet) of bringing one group of people into contact with another for the purpose of economic exchange. Perhaps the school could organise a market for the outside community; or one group within the school could make the physical arrangements for the market and deal with advertising and promotion, while another is responsible for production.

YOUNG PARTICIPATION

Making friends in the Bahamas.

YOUTH PARTICIPATION

Young people in the Commonwealth are in the majority. There are both official and unofficial organisations in the Commonwealth which aim to be of use to young people.

The Commonwealth Youth Programme is administered by the Commonwealth Secretariat and funded on a voluntary basis by member governments. It provides a wide range of services, including a Youth Project Fund which assists young people to establish projects of potential benefit to their communities - and at the same time creates employment opportunities for the young.

The Commonwealth Youth Exchange Council (see p.104) is an educational charity. It organises educational visits and exchanges between young people in Britain and other Commonwealth countries.

Activity 1: YOUTH PARTICIPATION AT SCHOOL AND IN THE COMMUNITY
Level: Secondary

Teachers can encourage students to participate in the running of their school. Students can find out how decisions are made in the school and what organisational structures exist. Could these structures be expanded and improved? Students can interview teachers, administrative staff and other students and draw up a proposal for a participatory framework.

How can the school be of use to the community? Are there ways in which young people can participate in local development? Students can talk to as a wide a range of people as possible, women and men, if possible tape-recording the interviews. They can discuss all the suggestions made and the problems raised and try to draw up a plan of action.

On Commonwealth Day

* **After permission has been sought from the interviewees, highlights from the tape could be played to visitors and a report on the community action/youth participation project could be given.**

Activity 2: WORK EXPERIENCE
Level: Mid-upper secondary

Young people leaving school may have few opportunities for employment. Unemployment is a growing problem for both Third World and industrialised countries. Schools can help students gain experience of the world of work, and opportunities to contribute to the development of their communities, by organising work experience schemes. Instead of having set ideas, perhaps unrealistic ones, about careers they wish to pursue, students can be encouraged to try out various possibilities, to investigate different ways of helping other people and themselves.

Teachers will need to make contact with local industries, businesses and services and discuss the possibilities, terms, conditions and responsibilities involved. Timetable changes may be necessary and long-term planning

will be required in order to avoid clashes with examinations and ensure
that the scheme causes minimum disruption. It will also be important to
devise ways of assessing the scheme and to allow students to discuss their
experiences, report back and make their own assessments.

Activity 3: DESIGN A PROJECT FOR THE YOUTH PROJECT FUND
                                                    Level: Upper secondary

This is really an extension of the last activity. Students who will soon
be leaving school could devise a project which will satisfy a community
need and which will involve young people in the economic, social or
cultural development of the community. If the idea is thought to be a
viable one (particularly if it creates employment and is potentially
self-sustaining), the school - or the group of young people - could try to
interest their government in applying for a small grant from the Youth
Project Fund to help the project get started. All applications to the
Youth Project Fund have to meet with the approval of the government and be
sent through the department responsible for youth affairs.

Some recent CYP Youth Project Awards

GHANA
National Youth Council

Manufacture of burnt bricks for rural areas

THE GAMBIA
Chosan Arts Projects

Traditional clothing design and manufacture

CYPRUS
Pan-Cyprian Co-ordination
Committee for Youth

Strovolos Youth Centre
Cultural Development Project

KENYA
Kenya Association of Youth Groups

Four carpentry and craft manufacture projects

MALAWI
Malawi Young Pioneers

Agricultural project involving six youth clubs

LESOTHO
Mesitaneng Youth Group

Egg production project

BANGLADESH
Jamalpur Youth Co-operative
Society

Dressmaking co-operative

SRI LANKA
National Youth Services Council

Handicraft production project

ZIMBABWE
Zimcare Trust

Project for mentally retarded to assist in decorating and maintenance

Further information on these projects can be obtained from the Commonwealth Youth Programme (see p.103).

On Commonwealth Day

* **Commonwealth Day is a good occasion for reporting back to the school and to visitors. Students' own records - in the form of diaries (photographs, tapes, reports) - are of particular importance. Local employers who have been co-operative and helpful could be invited to speak about the scheme from their point of view. Special initiatives, e.g. applications to the Youth Project Fund, should obviously be emphasised.**

8
COMMONWEALTH QUESTIONS

Commonwealth Day provides a good opportunity for posing questions about the Commonwealth - questions of fact and questions of value.

Activity 1: A COMMONWEALTH QUIZ   **Level: Junior/secondary**

Teachers (or a group of students) can compose a quiz based on the Commonwealth Day poster and map sent out each year by the Commonwealth Secretariat or on other information available to the school.

1. From the information given on the Commonwealth Day poster:

    -   how many countries belong to the Commonwealth?
    -   which countries have monarchies?
    -   which countries have republics?
    -   which countries have populations of less than one million people?
    -   which countries have populations of more than 50 million people?

2. From the information given on the Commonwealth Day poster name the countries which lie in:

    -   the Caribbean region
    -   the African region
    -   the Indian Ocean
    -   the Asian region
    -   the Australasian and South Pacific region
    -   the North American region
    -   the European region including the Mediterranean

3. From the information given on the Commonwealth Day poster name the countries of which the following towns and cities are the capitals:

    -   Port Louis
    -   Tarawa
    -   Castries
    -   Valetta
    -   Lusaka

4. From the information given on the Commonwealth Day poster name the Commonwealth countries that:

    -   lie wholly or partly on the equator
    -   are small island states
    -   are on Greenwich Mean Time (GMT)
    -   have a land boundary with another Commonwealth country

5. From the information given on the Commonwealth Day poster how many countries became members of the Commonwealth:

    -   between 1931 or before?
    -   between 1932 and 1959?
    -   between 1960 and 1969?
    -   between 1970 and 1979?
    -   since 1980?

Activity 2: DEBATES AND ESSAYS ON THE COMMONWEALTH   Level: Secondary

Commonwealth Day and the period of classroom work leading up to it should include plenty of opportunity, at least for the upper secondary level, to examine critically the Commonwealth's record. It is important for students to form their own opinions and to be confronted with attitudes and values different from their own.

Here are a few questions and statements to discuss in essay form or to debate:

"It is the inequalities among the members of the Commonwealth which are striking: the assumption of equality is a convenient fiction". (Paul Taylor, in The Commonwealth in the 80s).

President Nehru of India spoke of the Commonwealth being able to bring "a touch of healing" to a sick world. How far has his hope been fulfilled?

"Speaking English is a Commonwealth fact; it is not part of any Commonwealth ideology; it is one channel for easy communication, and a precious one in functional terms. It is not a badge of identity." (Shridath Ramphal). What do you think about the use of English in the Commonwealth and do you agree with Ramphal's view?

"Commonwealth might, in fact, be another word for communications" (Shridath Ramphal). Do you think this is a true equation?

Discuss the statement "The Commonwealth is more widely known today for its conferences than for its achievements".

How far do differences of opinion between Commonwealth countries weaken the power of the Commonwealth to influence world affairs?

The last two questions are taken from recent years' Royal Commonwealth Society essay competitions. Schools should be able to find out about this annual competition through the Commonwealth Desk Officer in their country's Ministry of Education or they can write to the Royal Commonwealth Society in London (see p.104).

(see p.104)

On Commonwealth Day

* **Any particularly interesting essay could be displayed on a school noticeboard.**

* **A debate could take place in front of (and involving the participation of) an audience of students, parents and visitors.**

9
FACTS AND FIGURES

MEMBERS OF THE COMMONWEALTH

Country	Capital	Area sq. km	GNP per capita US$ 1985	GNP per capita Av.ann. growth % 1973-85
Antigua & Barbuda	St John's	441	2,030	2.9
Australia	Canberra	7,686,848	10,840	1.4
Bahamas	Nassau	13,935	7,150	1.9
Bangladesh	Dhaka	143,998	150	2.0
Barbados	Bridgetown	431	4,680	1.5
Belize	Belmopan	22,963	1,130	-0.1
Botswana	Gaborone	600,372	840	6.4
Britain	London	244,046	8,390	1.1
Brunei Darussalam	Bandar Seri Begawan	5,765	17,580	-1.2
Canada	Ottawa	9,976,139	13,670	1.1
Cyprus	Nicosia	9,251	3,790	na
Dominica	Roseau	751	1,160	2.8
The Gambia	Banjul	11,295	230	-2.7
Ghana	Accra	238,537	390	-3.1
Grenada	St George's	344	970	na
Guyana	Georgetown	214.969	570	-2.3
India	New Delhi	3,287,590	250	2.0
Jamaica	Kingston	10,991	940	-3.5
Kenya	Nairobi	582,646	290	0.3
Kiribati	Tarawa	886	450(84)	-12.0
Lesotho	Maseru	30,355	480	-0.3
Malawi	Lilongwe	118,484	170	-0.4
Malaysia	Kuala Lumpur	329,749	2,050	4.3
Maldives	Male	298	290	3.3
Malta	Valletta	316	3,300	6.7
Mauritius	Port Louis	1,865	1,070	1.8
Nauru	Nauru	21	na	na
New Zealand	Wellington	268,676	7,310	0.7
Nigeria	Lagos	923,768	760	-2.5
Papua New Guinea	Port Moresby	461,691	710	-1.2
St Kitts and Nevis	Basseterre	269	1,520	0.0
St Lucia	Castries	616	1,210	2.9
St Vincent & Grenadines	Kingstown	388	840	2.3
Seychelles	Mahe	280	na	na
Sierra Leone	Freetown	71,740	370	-0.2
Singapore	Singapore	581	7,420	6.5
Solomon Islands	Honiara	28,446	510	na
Sri Lanka	Colombo	65,610	370	3.3
Swaziland	Mbabane	17,363	650	3.3
Tanzania	Dar es Salaam	945,087	270	-1.6
Tonga	Nuku'alofa	669	730	6.4
Trinidad & Tobago	Port of Spain	5,128	6,010	2.0
Tuvalu	Funafuti	28	na	na
Uganda	Kampala	236,036	230(84)	na
Vanuatu	Port Vila	11,880	700(84)	na
Western Samoa	Apia	2,842	660	na
Zambia	Lusaka	752,614	400	-2.6
Zimbabwe	Harare	390,580	650	0.0

Source: World Bank Atlas

SOCIAL DATA

Country	Population 1985	Population Density km (sq.km) 1985	Population under age 15 1982-85 (%)	Urban Population as % of total 1985
Antigua & Barbuda	78,000	177	37.7	30.8
Australia	15,789,000	2	24	87
Bahamas	234,000	17	38.7	66.1
Bangladesh	100,592,000	698	46	12
Barbados	252,000	585	28	42
Belize	159,000	7	46.7	49.8
Botswana	1,070,000	2	50.0	19
Britain	56,539,000	232	19.2	92
Brunei Darussalam	224,000	39	n.a.	na
Canada	25,414,000	2.5	26	75
Cyprus	660,000	71	25	50
Dominica	78,000	104	41.4	na
The Gambia	737,000	65	43	21
Ghana	12,710,000	53	47.0	40
Grenada	96,000	279	35.1	na
Guyana	806,000	4	37	32
India	765,147,000	232	37	26
Jamaica	2,227,000	203	37	54
Kenya	20,375,000	35	53	17
Kiribati	64,000	72	na	na
Lesotho	1,515,000	50	42	6
Malawi	7,044,000	59	48	12
Malaysia	15,611,000	47	37	32
Maldives	178,000	597	44.8	28.5
Malta	360,000	1,139	24	85
Mauritius	1,036,000	555	32	57
Nauru	8,000	380	na	na
New Zealand	3,246,000	12	25	84
Nigeria	99,669,000	108	48	23
Papua New Guinea	3,499,000	8	43	14
St Kitts and Nevis	43,000	160	37.4	na
St Lucia	136,000	221	47.7	na
St Vincent & Grenadines	119,000	307	38.3	na
Seychelles	65,000	232	37.4	na
Sierra Leone	3,745,000	52	41	28
Singapore	2,557,000	4,401	25	74
Solomon Islands	267,000	9	48.7	9.6
Sri Lanka	16,143,000	246	34	21
Swaziland	758,000	44	46	26
Tanzania	22,242,000	24	49	15
Tonga	97,000	139	na	na
Trinidad & Tobago	1,187,000	231	32	23
Tuvalu	8,000	286	na	na
Uganda	15,474,000	66	49	14
Vanuatu	134,000	11	45.2	25.5
Western Samoa	163,000	57	40.9	22.3
Zambia	6,640,000	9	47	50
Zimbabwe	8,406,000	22	48	25

SOCIAL DATA

Country	Women as % of total labour force 1982-85	Adult literacy (%) (1982-85)
Antigua & Barbuda	na	88
Australia	na	99
Bahamas	47.3[D]	93
Bangladesh	18.1	29
Barbados	43	99
Belize	na	91
Botswana	50.4	41
Britain	44.6	99
Brunei Darussalam	na	78
Canada	na	99
Cyprus	34.9	89
Dominica	34.9	94
The Gambia	43.4	20
Ghana	41.7	30
Grenada	42.0	98
Guyana	26.4	92
India	31.6	41
Jamaica	41.2	90
Kenya	33.6	47
Kiribati	na	na
Lesotho	44	52
Malawi	37.8	25
Malaysia	32.2	60
Maldives	37.1[B]	82
Malta	21.3	83
Mauritius	23.9	79
Nauru	na	na
New Zealand	na	99
Nigeria	40	34
Papua New Guinea	41.2	32
St Kitts and Nevis	na	98
St Lucia	na	82
St Vincent & Grenadines	36.3[C]	96
Seychelles	na	58
Sierra Leone	34.5	15
Singapore	26.2	83
Solomon Islands	na	na
Sri Lanka	25.6	86
Swaziland	45.7	65
Tanzania	36.2	79
Tonga	na	100
Trinidad & Tobago	32.5	95
Tuvalu	na	na
Uganda	33.7	52
Vanuatu	na	15
Western Samoa	16.7[A]	98
Zambia	33.3	44
Zimbabwe	39.2	69

Columns headed '1982-85' indicate that the figure given is for one year within the period.

Footnotes

A = 1976 C = 1978
B = 1977 D = 1980   na - not available

Sources

World Development Report 1987, The World Bank
Social Indicators Data Sheet June 1986, The World Bank
World Bank Atlas 1987
Unesco Yearbook 1987
Basic Statistical Data on Selected Countries, Commonwealth Secretariat 1986.

10
RESOURCES

RESOURCES

ORGANISATIONS

COMMONWEALTH SECRETARIAT
Marlborough House, Pall Mall, London SW1Y 5HX, UK.

COMMONWEALTH YOUTH PROGRAMME (CYP)
Headquarters - Commonwealth Secretariat, London.

Much of the CYP's work in helping governments to involve young people in national development is done through its four regional centres;

    CYP Africa Centre, P O Box 30190, Lusaka, Zambia.

    CYP Asia Centre, P O Box 78, Chandigarh, India.

    CYP Caribbean Centre, P O Box 101063, Georgetown, Guyana.

    CYP South Pacific Centre, University of the South Pacific, P O Box 1168, Suva, Fiji.

Regional organisations which often work closely with the Commonwealth include:

AFRICAN SOCIAL STUDIES PROGRAMME (ASSP)
P O Box 44777, Nairobi, Kenya.

ASSP has produced a Source book on Teaching and Learning About the Commonwealth Through Social Studies in Africa.

CARIBBEAN COMMUNITY SECRETARIAT (Caricom)
3rd Floor, Bank of Guyana Building, Georgetown, Guyana.

ECONOMIC COMMUNITY OF WEST AFRICAN STATES (Ecowas)
6 King George V Road, PMB 12745, Onikan, Lagos, Nigeria.

SOUTH PACIFIC COMMISSION
P O Box D5, Noumea Cedex, New Caledonia.

SOUTHERN AFRICAN DEVELOPMENT CO-ORDINATION CONFERENCE (SADCC)
P O Box 0095, Gaborone, Botswana.

There are hundreds of unofficial Commonwealth organisations. A few of these are listed below:

COMMONWEALTH INSTITUTE
Kensington High Street, London W8 6NQ, UK.

Educational organisation with permanent showcases of over 40 Commonwealth countries. Travelling exhibitions, cultural programmes, film, theatre. Conferences, courses and school programmes. Library and resource centre.

COMMONWEALTH INSTITUTE, SCOTLAND
8 Rutland Square, Edinburgh EH1 2AS, UK.

Operates independently of the Commonwealth Institute in London.
Conferences, school programmes, library and information services,
occasional exhibitions.

COMMONWEALTH LINKING TRUST
Second Floor, Seymour Mews House, 26-37 Seymour Mews, London W1H 9PE,
UK.

Links schools in the Commonwealth so that they may exchange
educational material, correspondence etc.

ROYAL COMMONWEALTH SOCIETY
18 Northumberland Avenue, London WC2N 5BJ, UK.

Works to promote understanding of the Commonwealth through
conferences, meetings and study visits. Organises an annual schools
essay competition, with travel and book prizes. Major library of
Commonwealth material, especially historical.

COMMONWEALTH YOUTH EXCHANGE COUNCIL
18 Fleet Street, London EC4Y 1AA, UK.

Promotes contact and exchanges between 15-25 year olds in the UK and
other Commonwealth countries.

COMMONWEALTH SOCIETY FOR THE DEAF
105 Gower Street, London WC1, UK.

ROYAL COMMONWEALTH SOCIETY FOR THE BLIND
Commonwealth House, Haywards Heath, West Sussex RH16 3AZ, UK.

Sponsors the world's largest programme of sight restoration and
blindness prevention through eye examinations and preventive and
education activities. Supports training for those working with the
blind.

COMMONWEALTH TRADE UNION COUNCIL (CTUC)
Congress House, 23-28 Great Russell Street, London WC1B 3LS, UK.

Promotes the interests of workers in Commonwealth countries through
co-operation between national trade union centres.

TANZANIA COMMONWEALTH SOCIETY
P O Box 6149, Arusha, Tanzania.

Promotes understanding of the Commonwealth through meetings,
lectures, educational programmes and information services.

UGANDA COMMONWEALTH SOCIETY
PO Box 7063, Kampala, Uganda.

Forum for discussion of national, international and Commonwealth
affairs. Supports programmes of social and economic development.

PUBLICATIONS

The Commonwealth Today, Commonwealth Secretariat, 48 pages, free. An introduction to the Commonwealth, areas of co-operation, the Secretariat non-governmental organisations etc.

Commonwealth Factbook 1987, Commonwealth Secretariat, 50 pages, £5. Basic geographical, political, social and economic data on all member countries, associated states and dependencies.

Commonwealth Skills for Commonwealth Needs, Commonwealth Secretariat, 49 pages, free. Describes the work of the Commonwealth Fund for Technical Co-operation (CFTC).

Mission to South Africa: The Commonwealth Report. The Findings of the Commonwealth Eminent Persons Group on Southern Africa. Penguin 1986, price £2.50

Racism in Southern Africa: the Commonwealth Stand, Commonwealth Secretariat, 50 pages, free. Excellent and very readable booklet charting events in South Africa, Namibia and Zimbabwe and the response of the Commonwealth. Well illustrated with b & w photos.

Commonwealth Organisations, Commonwealth Secretariat, 112 pages, price £4. A directory of official and unofficial organisations active in the Commonwealth.

Vulnerability: Small States in the Global Society, Commonwealth Secretariat, 126 pages, price £5.

The Commonwealth Secretariat will waive charges on orders from schools. It also produces free leaflets on its areas of work and on all the principal Agreements, Statements and Declarations made by Heads of Government. A full list of Secretariat publications is available from the Information Division. A bi-monthly magazine, **Commonwealth Currents,** is available free on request.

Child-to-child Programme, Institute of Child Health, 30 Guildford Street, London WC1N 1EH, UK. Set of materials describing simple practical ways in which older children can help younger children avoid disease and accidents and grow up healthy. Recommended. (NB. Some of the health activities described in this handbook come from the Child-to-child Programme).

Contact: A Handbook for Commonwealth Youth Exchange, Commonwealth Youth Exchange Council, 38 pages, £1. Written mainly for the British market but has been found useful elsewhere.

Commonwealth Day: A Resource Book for Schools by Rosalind Kerven, Commonwealth Institute, 39 pages. Written with British schools in mind but includes useful facts and figures; examples of Commonwealth stories, games, recipes; information on religions, languages, exports etc.

Commonwealth Today, lively news magazine published every two months. Subscription details from World of Information, 21 Gold Street, Saffron Walden, Essex UK, CB10 1EJ.

ANNEX LIST OF SCHOOL PROJECTS AND ACTIVITIES